STARING DOWN THE WOLF

MARK DIVINE

ST. MARTIN'S PRESS
NEW YORK

First published in the United States by St. Martin's Press,
an imprint of St. Martin's Publishing Group

www.stmartins.com

Library of Congress Cataloging-in-Publication Data

Names: Divine, Mark, author.
Title: Staring down the wolf : 7 leadership commitments that forge elite teams /
    Mark Divine.
Description: First edition. | New York : St. Martin's Press, [2020] | Includes index.
Identifiers: LCCN 2019044456 | ISBN 9781250231581 (hardcover) |
    ISBN 9781250231598 (ebook)
Subjects: LCSH: Leadership. | Teams in the workplace. | Success in business.
Classification: LCC HD57.7 .D5938 2020 | DDC 658.4/092—dc23
LC record available at https://lccn.loc.gov/2019044456

Our books may be purchased in bulk for promotional, educational, or business
use. Please contact your local bookseller or the Macmillan Corporate and
Premium Sales Department at 1-800-221-7945, extension 5442, or by
email at MacmillanSpecialMarkets@macmillan.com.

First Edition: March 2020

10 9 8 7 6 5 4 3 2 1

CONTENTS

CONTENTS

STARING DOWN THE WOLF

INTRODUCTION
ENTERING NEW TERRAIN

TAKE A DEEP BREATH, THEN THROW THE OLD MAP AND COMPASS OUT

Are you a CEO or key leader desperate to drive new revenue and profit because the shifting business and technology landscape has made the old maps of how to win in your industry obsolete? At the same time, your teams and culture are struggling under the crush of commitments and the constant chaos.

Your HR department is missing the mark, off-kilter because its personnel are trained to deal with humans as resources, not as human beings demanding to be treated as such. They were fine when it was just about hiring, measuring, promoting, and firing . . . maybe even conducting surveys and initiating sensitivity training. But they are challenged to develop leaders in ways that now count most—emotionally, morally, and spiritually.

Perhaps you are one of those young leaders who feels disengaged because you resent being treated as an asset—or worse, being led by an asshole. The typical large organization is biased toward endless process and tasks, with little time for cultivating a powerful culture, which is critical to navigating this new terrain. The business world can be like a battlefield, and your organization could be on its way to getting seriously wounded, or killed, as a result.

In the new battleground, the internal terrain of emotional power and mindset is where the creative energy to win will come from. Those require new developmental models to effectively deal with the rapid change and uncertainty. After the cold war, the US Army War College coined an acronym for the volatility, uncertainty, complexity, and ambiguity of the world—VUCA—which has gained some familiarity in executive suites since. To win the mission in VUCA, leaders will need a next-generation compass, one that helps them to navigate the peaks and valleys with emotional, moral, and spiritual strength. They will need to set their egos aside and subordinate their needs to the team and mission, to become "whole leaders" who operate from a world-centric, integrated consciousness. Becoming whole and self-evolving allows leaders to develop a profoundly deep connection with their team. And it will lead to more meaningful success for their organizations in a future that is already upon us.

These are skills leaders desperately need right now.

But your fear wolf stands in the way.

The fear wolf is a metaphor for what's holding you back emotionally—those deeply engrained fears, negative reactionary patterns, and biases. What do these hold you back from? They hold you back from receiving 100 percent buy-in and alignment from your team. And they hold you back from your true self.

This book is about helping you stare down your own fear wolf to overcome lingering negative conditioning so you can evolve to your fullest capacity. It's the only way to unlock your truly massive potential.

This new battlefield will simply not let you chase profit at the expense of people any longer. Your people and your culture *are* your "main thing" now. Everything else is subject to the winds of change, easily made irrelevant as those winds blow.

As a leader, you are not the victim of VUCA. You can't blame the market, the volatility, the competitors, the investors, or the customers. It's up to you to change, or be killed, in this new business climate. Consider yourself lucky that you aren't likely to actually get killed, which was not something that I counted on in the SEALs. You cannot let volatility, complexity, and numbing ambiguity freeze you in your tracks.

I have found in my work with leaders and teams that most have hit a wall in the last five years or so. All of a sudden they are starting to feel incompetent. At some point, what had worked for them was no longer relevant; the weapons they trained with now do no damage. Their professional skills, developed in business school, endless workshops and courses, and OJT (on-the-job training) simply aren't delivering the desired results. Though they see and feel the elements of this new battleground acutely, they don't know how to proceed.

Fight, flight, and freeze has set in among the allied business troops.

Where are the Eisenhowers and Pattons when you need then?

Sorry, there is no savior this time around. There is no outside transformational leader or consultant who can "fix this" for you, or anyone else.

The only transformational leader available is *you*.

You must transform. And you must also transform your team.

You can't keep doing things that aren't working and expect better results. This book won't give you a bunch of fancy strategies and shiny tactics to solve your issues. Instead, it will give you insights on how to develop your own, and your team's, character. That character will be exemplified by moral and spiritual courage, trust and trustworthiness, respect and respectability, excellence through self-leadership and adaptability, persistent growth, resiliency, and alignment around a shared purpose, vision, and mission. These are the seven commitments that will lead to total team engagement.

Developing these skills will require that you look deep within to overcome any negative qualities holding you back from your ability to tap your full intuition, creativity, and connection. Frankly, you can't pretend to be the perfect leader, with all the good qualities and none of the bad. Your peeps saw through that mask long ago. Equally important, you must stop casting your *shadow* onto your team. Your shadow is your negative conditioned behavior, most often linked to the emotionally traumatic experiences of your youth, which now harms relationships and your team's performance. It shows up as projection; transference; aggressive, passive-aggressive, or passive behavior; or just outright horrible communication skills. Your team will not trust or respect you fully until you do this work. Your shadow makes you the limiting factor in your own success.

The way through VUCA is to push yourself and your teams to embody the seven commitments in this book. When you do so, you will accelerate your growth to the highest stages of development and wholeness. This is accomplished through the self-awareness of your fear wolf shadow, and through a daily practice of self-mastery. That will allow you to clean up your emotional shadow issues, wake up to your essential nature as a spiritual being, and grow into a fully authentic leader. This is hard work, but it must be done. Your future and the future of your teams—perhaps even the future of humanity itself when you consider our collective global challenges—depend on it.

You must stare down the wolf of fear.

YOUR FIVE PLATEAUS

It is well known in developmental psychology that we operate with differing internal maps of reality. This makes leading complex because not only is the external terrain shifting due to VUCA, but the internal terrains of team members are different from ours as well, with inconsistent and differing reality maps! Most leaders ignore this truth because they haven't learned to recognize the different terrains, or they are trapped in an incomplete map and can't see the forest for the trees. It takes awareness of the dominant reality perspectives in order to activate self-transformation.

I have identified five distinct points of view that my executive clients identify with (these are their reality terrains and maps), which I have termed the Five Plateaus. These plateaus frame their world views, reactions to others and pet beliefs. The plateaus are each internally consistent world views, but are incomplete in scope of inclusiveness, or wholeness, until the fifth is reached, which integrates them all. Additionally, one's shadow elements will show up differently in each plateau and can negatively impact developmental growth. These plateaus are fluid, in that the leader can hold an intellectualized belief from one level but react with a subconscious shadow pattern at another. The good news is that through a disciplined practice, with a daily, weekly, and annual "battle rhythm," leaders can destroy their shadow and grow quickly to ascend to the fifth plateau—the whole or integrated stage of development. Another way of saying this is that integration at the fifth plateau brings a more expansive and inclusive awareness and world view, one that transcends and includes all the previous stages. This embodied wholeness unlocks greater connection, potential, performance, and sense of service. Of course, it also allows one to lead more effectively and achieve more success, significance, and contentment.

Leaders who take their evolution seriously and grow to this fifth plateau will see more and more clearly and release shadow. This work is not a one-time thing—it is ongoing and there is no tape to run through at a finish line. It is also accepted by experts that growth continues beyond the fifth plateau, but unfortunately only a small percentage of humanity will ever see that perspective in our lifetimes. This helps explain why society has created such caustic and violent conditions. Let's make it our mission to guide our teams and new leaders to this fifth plateau, transforming not just them but global culture in the process.

If you are familiar with the work of the American philosopher Ken Wilber, you will note his influence, as well as that of other developmental psychologists, in the Five Plateaus. I have been honored to study and work with Ken and some of his earliest acolytes. Ken is the creator of Integral Theory, which is a growth framework that pairs Western psychological with Eastern transpersonal developmental models for complete map of the human experience. That map includes both the subjective and objective aspects of the individual and the collective. Awareness of all of these domains is important because these internal reality maps, when made an object of self-study, can be psychoactive—meaning that the mere awareness of them prompts growth to include them.

As a nearly lifelong student of Zen, yoga, and the martial arts, with twenty years of therapy, I am finally coming to deeply understand what Ken means when he says that our mission as humans is to "wake up, grow up, and clean up so we can show up as our true selves." Waking up is the experience of separating from one's origin story, thoughts, and emotions to recognize one's eternal nature and unity with all things. Paths to waking up are found in all perennial spiritual traditions. Waking up is how we come to appreciate the awesome potential that lies within all of us. Growing up is different. This means to evolve to fuller and more inclusive stages of personal development, thereby accessing more inclusivenes and leadership capacity. Finally, cleaning up is doing the emotional shadow work—which is the hard part—staring down the wolf of fear. Giving you the inspiration and tools to clean up, so you can continue to grow into greater leadership authenticity at the fifth plateu, is the purpose of this book.

WHAT'S YOUR PLATEAU?

Your own stage of development will be heavily influenced by the stage of your parents and the culture you grew up in. Those with ideal origin circumstances can develop naturally through the first four stages, or plateaus, which mirror the development of overall human consciousness itself through the industrial age. As mentioned, when people progress through each plateau, their sense of self and others gets more expansive and inclusive. The first plateau is pure egocentric, with a focus solely on self-needs. The second is ethnocentric with a focus on the tribe, while the third is largely ethnocentric but has the potential to be world-centric for those involved in global travel and work. The fourth and fifth plateaus are world-centric oriented, displaying increasing care and concern for all humans and the planet itself. Unfortunately, Wilber estimates that around 5 percent of the world's population is at the fifth.

The following Five Plateau graphic offers a map of each stage:

Plateau	Attitudes and Development Stages	Archetypal Postures	Positive Emotions & Motivations	Reactionary Shadow
1st	• Primary attitude: Survivor • Developmental stage: Egocentric	• Survival of the fittest • Independent.... I got mine • Risk taker • Lone wolf or Con artist • Gang member • Security needs not met	• Bold action • Love (contracted) • No quitting	• Rashness • Shame or Pride • Aggression or Submission • Anxiety • Lack trust or respect • Fixed mindset • Excessive risk taking
2nd	• Primary attitude: Protector • Developmental stage: Ethnocentric with extreme focus on one's tribe	• Warrior/Sheepdog • Fundamentalist and traditionalist with regards to family, religion and roles: the old way still the best way • Bureaucratic—rules, position, and rank very important Security and limited resources must be protected	• Courageous action • Trust and respect for authority, traditional roles • Protect the status quo • Fight for right • Love of tribe. Patriotism • Trust in a higher power and role of religion	• Guilt • Jealousy • Low self-worthiness • Fixed mindset "that's just the way it's done" • "ism's"—racism, sexism, ageism, etc. • Hierarchical rigidity
3rd	• Primary attitude: Achiever • Developmental stage: Ethnocentric (capitalism better than communism) also emerging worldcentric via global trade and solving problems via tech	• Leader, Entrepreneur, Executive, Professional • Self-Reliant and Independent • Material success focus • Merit more important than rank and position	• Trust in ability to create • Ambition, gets things done • Team player to meet their needs • Seek horizontal growth—personal development for success • First five commitments present	• Careless • Reckless • Greedy • Abstract thought and moral relativism
4th	• Primary attitude: Equalizer • Developmental stage: Worldcentric, ecology, activism, sustainable commercialism, conscious capitalism. philanthropy	• Social Entrepreneur, Academic, Non-profit leader • Sensitive, Egalitarian, • Activist, Philanthropist • Acts from Caring, Concern, Scarcity	• Seven Commitments present, but not integrated • Respect equality • Caring, building relationships • Love and healing others • Seeking vertical growth—development for service • Opening to mystery of universe	• Spiritual Egotism • Class Envy or Anger • Lack of inclusiveness of others, i.e.: those deemed beneath their level of development or intelligence • Lack of concrete action—abstract save the world type thinking
5th	• Primary attitude: Integrator • Developmental stage: Worldcentric, commercialism with needs of all of humanity, and Earth taken into consideration. Gaia as a living system requiring all species to be in balance	• Global strategist or thought leader • Integrated Healer • Master teacher...., i.e.: Yogi, Chi Gong, Aikido, Integrated Unbeatable Mind Coach • Focus on Process and interdependence of systems • Thinks Win-Win, acts from Compassion, Abundance, Generosity, Service	• Integration of 7 Commitments • Strong vision • Embodiment—experience the world in different ways... body mind, spirit, vision, action • Wholeness, peace, and balance • Manages complexity • Universal care and concern	• Hyper-focus on development • Can be too inclusive and miss the trees within the forest • Can be narrow-minded in thinking everyone is right • Residual spiritual egotism • Lack skills to meet others from the perspective of their respective plateaus

Note: For those familiar with the work of Wilber, you will see that I have deliberately conflated his first three levels into the survivor plateau. These early three relate to archaic, magic, and mythic levels of growth, which are not often seen in successful leaders in the West. Generally, we see mostly second, third, and fourth plateau leadership perspectives.

As mentioned, leaders and teams have the capacity for all five plateaus, but usually level out at one of the plateaus, though they won't recognize it—they are inside the bottle and can't read the label. It may be apparent to others but not to them because they are not familiar with the maps. And many will lack the knowledge, desire, time, opportunity, or energy to work toward this important character growth. Most people are comfortable at their respective plateaus. Their relationships as well as political, religious, and other views make sense from that vista. And they are not wrong—just incomplete. Ignorance truly is bliss in this sense. It is comfortable to stay in their comfort zone and will not budge if they are unmotivated, overburdened, chemically depressed, numbed out, or in outright survival mode. Nor will they be inclined to grow if they are deeply ensconced in their tribe and its stories. They may be unwilling to consider the views, or even lives, of others as having equal relative worth. This is the classic *fixed mindset* that Carol Dweck, in her excellent book *Mindset,* speaks of. A fixed mindset is not uncommon in teams—as shadow work and integral leadership are new ideas for most leaders. Because you are reading this book, I assume you are not of a fixed mindset and are keen to grow—and grow fast.

Even if we have a growth mindset, it is statistically likely we are not all at the fifth plateau, so consider that you have room to grow! I was in a developmental rut for years due to my own incomplete map and the shadows that kept me in the third plateau achiever and second plateau protector modes. Daily self-awareness training, and staring down my fear wolf, allowed me to break those self-imposed limitations and progress to the highest stage of my own evolution.

Now it is time for you to wake up, grow up, clean up, and show up for your team! Question: *What plateau do you most identify with now?*

You may find that in your finest moments, you identify with the fifth plateau—peaceful and loving toward all—but when your fear wolf howls, you are pulled back to the third plateau—as an insensitive hyperachiever—or the second plateau, emotionally embroiled in your football team's loss to the point that you are raving mad and nearly engage in a fistfight.

As mentioned, your upbringing and shadow aspects will highly influence your development through these plateaus, and those are not something you had much control over. It is important not to judge yourself, feel put down, or take this as a value hierarchy ranking. Nobody gets graded in personal development. In fact, reacting that way would be normal and a sign that you have work to do. The first step in growing up and cleaning up is to draw awareness to the incomplete maps and shadow elements holding you back. Then you can train until full integration occurs—in a "transcend and include" manner. In the process you will get more skilled at how to navigate between the plateaus as you experience different people and circumstances. By staring down the wolf, you will find your awareness evolves further as shadow aspects from each plateau are released.

STARING DOWN THE WOLF

To summarize, staring down the wolf means facing your deepest negative conditioned qualities, or fears, and then staring them down to reduce their impact on your life. You must starve them out so they don't hold back your growth and full integration at the fifth plateau. As you do this, you will become the most impactful leader possible.

As mentioned, the shadow aspects of your being are the biases, subconscious patterns, and reactionary behaviors that sabotage your best efforts and tarnish relationships. You have them whether you like to admit it or not, and they prevent you from being that heart-centered leader you desire to be.

Through a long journey of self-discovery, which I will share with you in these pages, I have found my success as a leader, especially in navigating VUCA, has been dramatically enhanced by eradicating my own shadow conditioning. That has led to great authenticity, which then allowed me to build elite teams operating with the seven commitments in this book. And these commitments are also the qualities that I had to fully embody myself. One must lead by example in matters of the heart.

Many of the fears we experience in life are those of an existential nature—mainly, fear of death, or from a SEAL's perspective, fear of dark underwater spaces. But others such as fear of risk, of failure, judgment, discomfort, uniqueness, or obstacles, are related to childhood trauma shadow feelings of abandonment, insecurity, irrelevance, or unworthiness. There are tactics to deal with the first type of raw fear, and many of us employ them. But those brute force tactics of emotional control do not help much with the second type of fear, the shadow type. Those patterns will keep resurfacing to sabotage your progress. Examples of shadow issues as they expose themselves at each plateau can include:

■ **FIRST PLATEAU:** Playing victim to your trauma; short-term survival thinking; behaving impulsively; being overly superstitious or ritualistic; being vindictive; shaming others and being easily shamed; exhibiting passive-aggressive and addictive behavior; feeling insecure, not seen, not valued, unworthy. Reclusive or feeling disconnected to others.

■ **SECOND PLATEAU:** Taking on guilt effortlessly and guilting others; being jealous of the success, body, wealth, or position of others; exhibiting aggressive, passive-aggressive or controlling behavior; generating moral absolutisms; posturing. Arrogant, racist, sexist, or with extreme religiosity.

■ **THIRD PLATEAU:** Being hypercompetitive or materialistic; exhibiting workaholism, recklessness, greed, or excessive risk taking; not wanting any help—going it alone feels safer; avoiding conflict and crucial conversations; needing to be admired—Mr. or Ms. Perfect.

■ **FOURTH PLATEAU:** Exhibiting hypersensitivity; sweeping important issues under the rug due to emotional discomfort in dealing with them; judging those you don't agree with; forcing your fourth plateau views on others or on the collective as the right and only way.

■ **FIFTH PLATEAU:** Dealing with awareness of lingering shadow from other plateaus; tending to transfer mother and father issues onto the opposite sex or authority figures; projecting what you dislike or have disowned in yourself onto others.

As I have hammered home, these are the shadow fears that can cripple your leadership capacity. Why? Because everyone on your team feels the dysfunction acutely. Additionally, they are equally imperfect and know that you are human like them. If you pretend to be otherwise while dropping grenades of negativity on them, you lose them immediately. The team becomes paralyzed and disengaged, settling into mediocrity.

Here are some of the fear wolf patterns that impacted my own leadership capacity, and the root causes of them:

■ I did not feel smart as a young adult, so I went after advanced degrees that didn't do much for me. I needed to prove to myself and others that I was, in fact, smart. In leadership roles, I always had to be right; I had to have the last word and was not very inclusive of the viewpoints of others. This lack of confidence in my intellectual capacity was related to how, as a child, I took on a negative self-concept due to conditioning from my parents.

■ I was shut down emotionally in early life by abusive behavior and poor relationship modeling in the home. I was withdrawn as a result, which led to relationship drama as I went from one failed relationship to another. Bringing that lack of emotional awareness into leadership roles was a problem.

■ I learned to be codependent as a young adult and was anointed (perhaps self-appointed) the perfect one, so I always presented as squared away. This meant that I said yes to practically everything, and everyone. As a leader, I had trouble saying no, and couldn't evaluate well what (and who) were a good fit for me. This led to an enormous energy drain disengaging from bad commitments, and from ejecting narcissists who were taking advantage of me.

- I did not trust my innate wisdom and worthiness. As a result, I was intimidated by authority figures and jealous of those who appeared more successful. This further fueled the need to constantly prove myself.

- Feeling perpetually discontent with my development, I sought to constantly "fix myself" with a relentless pursuit of personal, professional, and spiritual development.

SEAL training and years of meditation hadn't eradicated all that negative conditioning, which had blocked my further growth. I was locked in second and third plateau thinking for years.

I had to stare down my wolf of fear, and do the shadow work to break free.

In spite of all that conditioning, by staring down the wolf I have been blessed to grow with a happy family, build successful businesses, launch a top-ranked podcast and author several bestselling books. I admitted my flaws, upgraded my map, and went to work on the shadow issues. Only after that work would I finally show up authentically for my teams. They wanted and deserved this, and when

I was able to connect to them deeply and humbly, they responded in kind. After working with many successful executives, entrepreneurs, and other hotshots, I can tell you confidently that everyone has similar fear wolf baggage—and they are so much more effective and happier when they do this work!

THE WOLVES WITHIN

The analogy of the fear wolf comes from a Native American tale of a negative wolf that resides in the mind of humans. This wolf operates from fear, is hungry for drama, catastrophizes, and has incessant negative self-talk.

But there is a second, positive wolf residing in the heart. This one has an appetite for love and connection, is not addicted to drama, and is optimistic and focused on others.

The fear wolf fights for your attention and demands dominance. The courage wolf asks simply to be noticed, seeking some esteem-building food. According to the legend, the one that ultimately controls you is the one you feed the most.

If you constantly feed fear by thinking about the could-haves, the should-haves, the would-haves, and the can'ts in life—if you allow negative beliefs, attitudes, and conditioned behavior from whatever drama you experienced or stories you adopted—then the fear wolf gets stronger. Eventually he gets so strong that the courage wolf is left cowering, unable to fight back.

However, you can stare that fear wolf down and refuse to feed it any longer. Starve it of that negative conditioning! Then you can feed the courage wolf a steady diet of good food, and lead with your heart and mind as equal partners.

Now, in case you are saying to yourself, *Well, crap, I thought this was going to be a book about cool Navy SEAL leadership strategies, but here we are talking psychobabble.*

Rest assured, I am going to go there. The main thrust of the book will be about how others have stared down their fear wolves to display the seven commitments in action. But I will also show you where I have failed and then learned to embody the commitments myself. I will give you a path to the freedom that lies on the other side of fear.

If my personal journey to leadership authenticity sounds tortuous and winding after reading about it, it's because it was. My hope is that after you employ the tools in this book, you won't have to become a SEAL, or do twenty-five years of meditation and twenty years of therapy, before finding your own authenticity. You will get there much faster, building elite teams and leading from the fifth plateau. You will become a heart-centered, world-centric leader by getting serious about the seven commitments *with your team*. You will train and develop a culture of excellence together and unlock more potential than you can now imagine.

That is how you will conquer the VUCA battleground.

The simple secret is to evolve your character to be worthy of leading other leaders.

Staring down the wolf is your new mantra—getting out of your head and into your heart. Only then can you move beyond your limitations and build a team capable of twenty times more.

This work is easier said than done. But you can trust me on this: it is 100 percent worth it.

Your team is waiting for you to show up.

A note about the stories in the book: The stories about military leaders told herein are meant to illustrate the seven commitments. They come from my direct observation or were related to me by teammates. The stories are not drawn from historical archives and are not likely to be perfectly accurate reflections of their respective events. Having said that, I assure you they are accurate to the best of my knowledge. I am most interested in how the stories illustrate the principle that I'm discussing.

FEAR: FAILURE EXPECTED. ARE YOU READY?

YOU'RE NOT PERFECT, I'M NOT PERFECT. SO WHAT?

I took certain things for granted when I was a young leader

in the SEALs. This became evident when my first attempt at

building a team in the world of business was an unmitigated

disaster.

Prior to the SEALs I had an abbreviated career in the

corporate world, where I was as clueless as everyone else as to what made a good team. I was just another cog in the wheel, but I did keep my eyes wide open searching for best practices. Though I couldn't articulate it—what was a good team and what was a bad team—at the age of twenty-one, I knew I didn't like what I was seeing.

What I saw—working for large companies like Arthur Andersen, Coopers & Lybrand, and Paine Webber—was a great deal of self-serving behavior. Aligned teams, a culture of excellence, and moral character got no attention. Employees were concerned with saving their own hide, improving their relative positions while ignoring the impact they could have on the culture or the organization. Only one of those firms is still in existence today, so it's safe to say that the others experienced a failure of leadership.

I felt no connection to my teams there, and the cultures were not in sync with the utopian ideas I held about leadership. My focus even then was not so much on external things—money, homes, or toys. I was looking for a more purpose-driven sense of self and a more visceral experience of leading. Becoming a real leader in that corporate setting seemed like a long shot, though I could see myself as a good manager, working out a way to climb the corporate ladder. Once I had put in enough time and had the tactical skills, I'd get the promotions and more peeps to manage.

It was not very inspiring, to say the least.

So I bailed and joined the U.S. Navy SEALs.

I mean, why not, right?

BEGINNER'S MIND

The four years I spent as an MBA and CPA on Wall Street was not all lost time. After all, I came into direct contact with the great wisdom tradition of Zen, which changed my life. Under the watchful eye of Master Tadashi Nakamura, I took to Zen like a baby to its mother's breast. The training allowed me to take control over my unruly mind and become aware that the mental loops I was running, programmed by my family and small-town upbringing, were in desperate need of an upgrade. Zen provided that upgrade through the daily practice, where I was slowly *waking up* and accessing the new terrain and map that would guide my future growth.

I was meeting my true self for the first time.

After I had tamed my mind somewhat, the next order of business was to explore the internal stories driving behavior that weren't serving me well—and that was most of them. As I did that, my self-concept began to expand dramatically: I found myself more creative, responsive, and spontaneous. I could see my future more clearly and did not react as negatively to life's challenges. This was a humbling and liberating period of my life. In retrospect, I was achieving the "beginner's mind" that the Zen master spoke of.

At age twenty-five, I emptied my cup of most of the irrelevant business stuff I had learned and flew across the country to become a Navy SEAL officer—and a real leader.

At BUD/S (Basic Underwater Demolition/SEAL Training), I was with a group of hard chargers seeking the biggest challenge they could find. Immediately, I could see that they were all aspiring leaders like me. Also, I saw that the organization was methodical in the way it developed its leaders and teams. It was drastically different from the Wall Street I had experienced months earlier, as if I had landed on a different planet and was learning from a new species. The SEALs were very focused on the *growing-up* aspect of developing young leaders, while the *cleaning up* of emotional baggage was up to the individuals. Some of that would come as the result of getting smacked down by your screw-ups.

I was put in charge of a small team called a boat crew, named so because we went everywhere with boats on our heads. The boats were called the IBS, which stands for "*Inflatable Boat, Small*," but I was told it was for *Itty-Bitty Ship*. The SEALs love humor to take their minds off the constant stress! I emphasized to my team that we were all in this together, and that although I was their appointed leader, I intended to be a team player first and to help each of them get to graduation day. We adopted the attitude that the instructors were going to have to kill us all to get us out of there. If at any moment they felt the urge to quit, they agreed to get with me or another teammate to help them through it. This was different from the way I was treated in the corporate world, and it felt good—like we were leading from our hearts and not our heads.

BUD/S (with the follow-on SEAL Qualification Training, or SQT) is a nine-month selection course designed to weed out those who don't have the leadership character to be on the SEAL teams. That meant the character to lead the self, the character to lead others, and the character to be led. The training is constantly checking all three of those aspects of character. Candidates who lacked any of the three quickly quit or were weeded out, and boat crews reorganized almost daily. The point of the training was obvious to me, and it wasn't to prove how tough we were—toughness was a prerequisite. The point was to prove one's willingness to grow to be both a good leader and a good teammate.

I started BUD/S class 170 with a hundred and eighty-five absolute studs. By the end of our training, there were only nineteen leaders left. All seven of my boat crew were standing tall with me—big smiles on graduation day. And I was voted the honor man of the class.

Without fully understanding how or why I had done it, I had built my first elite team—one that had the capacity to endure the most demanding physical, mental, and emotional training in the world. Each teammate had displayed courage, created trust, fostered respect, and grown better, while continuing to focus on our mission.

I repeated that experience many times as a leader in the SEALs. I thought I had figured out how to be an authentic leader. So when I left active duty to start my first business, it stood to reason that I'd have no problems replicating that level of success, right?

Hardly.

FAILING FAST

Before I left the active duty SEALs for the reserves in 1996, I formed my first entrepreneurial venture. The plan was for a brewpub in the SEALs' hometown of Coronado, California, called the Coronado Brewing Company, or CBC for short (the Navy must have drilled in me the need for another acronym). My brother-in-law, whom I was just getting to know and who had won me over with the idea of doing a bar business together, was to be my business partner.

Naturally, it made complete sense that this venture would involve beer. I grew up with beer and had another master's degree in drinking it. Alcohol was part of my family of origin shadow that would soon provide more fuel for my fear wolf. Business-wise, craft beer was an excellent opportunity, and we were early in the space as the fourth brewery in San Diego. I didn't put much thought into the why behind this idea. Owning a brewery sounded pretty freaking awesome to me.

Maybe you can appreciate that.

Anyway, I certainly had no desire to go back to a large corporate job or to my family's business in Upstate New York. And the SEALs had given me a lot of confidence to strike out on my own, so though I knew nothing about making beer, running a restaurant, or starting a business, for that matter, I knew that I could *find a way or make one,* as we were fond of saying in the teams.

My partner wasn't willing to run day-to-day operations because he had another business to tend to. I had to decide whether to leave the Navy to take that role on. I was seeing how challenging SEAL life was going to be as a married guy and reflected that if the Navy had wanted me to have either a wife or a business, they would have issued both to me. I grudgingly left the excitement and camaraderie of my elite SEAL team to take on the role as CEO of CBC.

Welcome to a new battlefield, Mark.

I put my *no-quit badge* on my sleeve and went to work. I thought that my SEAL focus and proven leadership skills would be the secret sauce for my success. Armed and ready, I liquidated my small IRA and raised $600,000 in seed capital from my family and teammates. Then with my previously hard-earned MBA and CPA and a business plan in hand, I secured an additional $800,000 loan from the Small Business Administration. We closed on the real estate and got the place built like a SEAL op, opening the doors with a massive party six months after I left the active duty Navy.

Mission accomplished!

Hardly. The insurgency started soon after.

I'd learned in the SEALs about the importance of engaging targets while not losing sight of the big-picture team needs. Also, to make sure I was clear on the why of the mission and maintained a clear vision of the battlefield. Constantly checking in on and realigning with those things had been drilled into me. But somehow in this new battlefield of the corporate world, I didn't do that. Something was missing. I was so focused on the constant crush of cash-flow and operational needs that I couldn't see the changing battleground. I didn't have my elite SEAL team to check my six (a military term meaning *look behind me*) and improve my thinking. The selection, training, culture, and systems of the SEALs were not backing me up now. Instead, I faced a "tabula rasa" day in and day out—a blank slate—filling up fast with negative bullshit.

My fear wolf was licking his chops.

Before we even opened the doors, my partner made his first power move. He declared that he was bringing his brother onto the team as a full equity partner. My codependent mind offered no objection. Why? Because codependence was a big shadow issue of mine. Suddenly there were the "three brothers" who started the Coronado Brewing Company—with me as the outsider (in their minds). We brewed a beer named Three Brothers Pale Ale, and I just kept moving forward.

Just like that, my ownership stake and voting power went from 50 percent to 33 percent, which after dilution from outside shareholders was closer to 20 percent. I had put in all my savings, raised all the outside capital, and was the full-time CEO. My partners put none of their own money in at that point, didn't raise a dime, and didn't work full-time in the business day to day.

What was I thinking, you ask?

Good question. With no recognition at all of what was going on, I had started the business with my third plateau achiever self, but was acting out negative conditioning from my first plateau survivor and second plateau protector shadow. I kept hoping for things to be different, but it slowly dawned on me that I had some bad teammates pulling me down. I simply didn't have the skills to navigate their manipulation, so I would need to fight my own teammates— and I was failing at that.

I was definitely uncovering some blind spots, and began to see that my fear wolf was ruling my inner wolf pack.

By not being clear on what I stood for and then standing that ground, I had established a new, lower standard. That standard was to let my brothers-in-law define the rules of engagement and the organization's culture by default. Staying in my strengths by focusing solely on tactical operations while ignoring the seven commitments of this book, I allowed them to negatively infect the entire company.

I did not confront them directly because avoiding conflict was part of the fear conditioning that I had not yet dealt with. So, I went to the board of directors with confessions of a leadership team gone to shit.

They would handle it, I hoped.

Not a chance. That just perpetuated the dysfunction. My partners received the news back channel and immediately assumed war battle footing, lining up their stories and battle plan. Meanwhile, the business was running short on capital, so I brought in another big investor to shore things up and—incredibly enough—began to expand the business.

When the brothers told me flat out that they would vote against expansion and instead wanted to buy out investors at a deep discount, I finally admitted to myself that we had a real gap in our views and standards. This was suddenly more than a personality conflict. I tried to get them to buy in on my vision and to ensure the investors would get a generous return on investment.

No go.

Instead, they mounted an all-out campaign against me, forcing investors and family members to take sides. In a fight for the valuable asset, they estranged their sister (my wife) as well as their father, a former Marine who was supportive of my efforts to protect the shareholders. Their self-proclaimed "scorched earth campaign" drove a wedge between family members that has not healed to this day.

What an epic fail.

I tried to sell the business, but nobody would touch it with all the legal entanglements. My wife begged me to walk away, so I finally threw in the towel and negotiated a buyout with the brothers—at far less than the company was worth—and walked away. I had built and handed them a business that was worth millions.

It pays to be a nice guy, right?

Riiight.

Despite all of my training in confronting an enemy head on, I lacked the skills to see my own emotional gaps and confront my deepest subconscious fears. That failure of leadership was predominantly due to my reactive conditioning, not to my tactical skills. Negative conditioning from my upbringing—the shadows I spoke of earlier that I had never dealt with—tripped me up. And as I have found out in my work since CBC with thousands of leaders and hundreds of teams, negative conditioning is the *main* reason that they fail as well.

This case study shows the soft underbelly of leadership that few want or even know how to address. No matter how smart and skilled you are, it is your stage of development and emotional awareness that will define your character as a leader. And your character will define how the team responds to you. If you have unresolved negative conditioning, you will not succeed at the level you aspire to.

And *all* leaders I have observed have some level of unresolved negative conditioning that they are not aware of. It leads to one obstacle or failure after another. These are taken in stride as "life lessons." Failure is to be expected. Are you ready for it?

BECOME A LEADER OF LEADERS

What you see on TV is that the SEALs excel in training the fun stuff—the tactical skills—of swimming an ungodly number of miles in the ocean with sharks all around, shooting things from a mile away, blowing shit up, jumping out of perfectly good airplanes, going around corners fast in high-speed boats, crossing enemy beaches effortlessly, and nailing the worst of the bad guys with a smile.

However, what they don't show is the considerable time spent developing the skills of mental and emotional control. Brutal honesty is standard operating procedure (SOP), which ensures that remediation happens immediately after a standard is breached. Things are not swept under the rug, and the temporary discomfort of dealing with emotionally charged issues is always deemed better than the long-term pain of ignoring them.

In the SOF (special operations forces) world, everyone is both a leader and a teammate. The leaders lead teams of leaders. Everyone carries his or her weight and character is deemed king. In any role, even that of commanding officer of a team, if you are the source of dysfunction and can't overcome your shortcomings, you are invited to leave. This happens from the earliest stages of selection and training and continues for an entire career. Emotional control is developed through your mess-ups. The structure of the organization forces some level of character development. The radical focus on the character of the individual and the culture of the team is fundamental to the SOF community's success.

But clearly special operators are not perfect and exhibit the same human faults as everyone else. I certainly did, and so did all of my teammates. Everyone struggles with their fear wolf—no matter how well trained they are in controlling their minds and emotions. Suppressing emotions, which was valuable as a warrior, has limited use as a corporate leader. And it is considerably easier to learn emotional control than to develop awareness of a shadow issue and then resolve it. Additionally, though the special ops community is good at developing mental toughness, they are behind the curve on how to develop cognitive performance and moral character. There is an ongoing discussion in the SEALs about whether moral character can be trained at all, and if so, how. I believe that only by helping individuals access new reality maps to become more self-aware and whole can they cultivate their own moral character.

However, even though many leaders and teams in the special ops battlefield fail on character flaws, as a whole, the force dominates the enemy. That is because the organization is structured to shape culture around the seven commitments profiled in this book. When the structure of an organization can shape the courage, trust, respect, growth, excellence, resiliency, and alignment of its individuals and teams, then it is much more likely to rout out issues arising from the negative conditioning of any individual leader. The organization becomes resilient and responsive to volatility, rather than reactionary to it. It is confident amid uncertainty. It is fluid and can navigate complexity. It will fail forward fast to deal with ambiguity. That is how special ops deal with VUCA.

My first entrepreneurial team-building experience with CBC was painful, but it also caused me to step back and ask myself, *What the hell went wrong?* I saw that what went wrong lay deep within me, and it limited my moves externally. I decided then to make the study of integrated development, and emotionally aware leadership, my life's work.

It would have been far more comfortable for me to open this book with a story of what a badass Navy SEAL leader I was to accompany the other stories of elite SEALs leading elite teams in the book. However, I have learned over time that guiding leaders and teams on the battlefields of the corporate world is harder than in the special ops world. I learned more about authentic leadership from my civilian screw-ups than I ever did in the military.

Failure is to be expected. Be ready for it.

SDTW Exercise 1:
RUTHLESS SELF-ASSESSMENT

Take a moment to assess the fear wolf shadow issues that have shown up in your own life. Grab your journal, practice deep diaphragmatic breathing with your eyes closed for a few minutes to clear your head, and then answer with brutal honesty the following questions:

1. What issues do you *know* for sure are patterns of yours that have impacted:

    a. Your fitness and health

    b. Your personal relationships, including significant others

    c. Your professional relationships to those above, below, and around you

2. Review the list in the introduction. What issues do you *suspect* are part of your fear wolf shadow system?

    a. First Plateau

    b. Second Plateau

    c. Third Plateau

    d. Fourth Plateau

    e. Not able to categorize, but you know it is there

3. Now commit to do the work in this book, and never, ever quit until you are firmly settled in at the fifth plateau and accelerating beyond!

LEADERSHIP COMMITMENT
#1

COMMIT TO
COURAGE

STARE DOWN THE FEAR OF RISK

Courage is the most important of all the virtues. Without that
virtue you can't practice any other virtue with consistency.
—"Maya Angelou, The Art of Fiction No. 119," *The Paris Review*

It was October of 1993 when the United States was trying to

bring stability to Somalia.

Our forces were in Mogadishu, working with a warlord

named Mohamed Farrah Aidid on a peacekeeping support

mission. We had one joint special operations task force stationed at the UN peacekeeping compound, staffed with the 75th Ranger Regiment—along with a bevy of communicators, administrators, intelligence officers, and logistics folks. There was a small contingent of other special ops on site, one of whom was SEAL leader Eric Olson.

The Rangers routinely patrolled the city in a show of presence, as well as to search for hidden weapon caches and bad guys. One day the situation with Aidid suddenly broke down, and the city devolved into a Wild West VUCA shootout. Just about every Somali in Mogadishu had a weapon—including the young kids. A weapon in someone's hands was as common as a cup of coffee there, and as easily accessible. The residents slung guns over their shoulders like yoga mats. One detail was that most of them had no training in using these weapons. There were countless instances of individuals shooting friends, even themselves, by mistake.

It was pure lawlessness.

The Rangers were on patrol when called to respond to a helicopter grounding. The pilots needed an extract. The disaffected locals began taking shots at both the Rangers and the pilots—and it soon turned into life-and-death combat for all of them. As so often happens in situations like these, the sound of gunfire attracted more of the gun-toting Somali "freedom fighters" like moths to the flame.

Before long, it seemed every local with a gun was running toward the firefight.

The Rangers are highly trained warriors, but this situation was not in the *Ranger Handbook*. Though it's in their team DNA to shoot, move, communicate, and dominate, they soon got overwhelmed and were taking casualties. Men were wounded and without medical attention were going to bleed out. The pilots were not faring any better, and their unfortunate plight was what later became the basis for the movie *Black Hawk Down*.

The story behind the story, however, has not often been heard. This is how the small elite SOF team stood their ground by staring down their fear wolf.

Back at the Joint SPEC OPS headquarters, where the United Nations peacekeeping force was stationed, there was a quick reaction force, or QRF. This unit was from an allied nation's military and was to assist in any crisis in an ongoing mission. The QRF had armored personnel carriers and were ready to go the moment they got the call.

At that moment, the Rangers called.

And . . . the QRF stayed put.

There is an ironclad American military ethos that you never leave teammates in the field in danger. You do what you can, even at great risk, to support or rescue them. The QRF force apparently did not share that ethos. They deemed the situation as extremely risky—which it definitely was. Regardless, their leadership team elected to keep the QRF team safe and sound in the compound, while the Rangers fought furiously to get to safety.

The SEAL officer and the other American forces watched this scenario unfold with distress. They had been forged to lead by example; in the midst of a crisis, these trained warriors were the ones to step into the breach. There were three other elite special operators in the compound—another Navy SEAL and two Delta Force operators. Olson's assessment was simple: they could watch the Rangers die or get into the fight and help them out.

Easy one.

The good news was that the Somali shooters had zero training. The bad news was that there were, quite literally, hundreds of them. Four more Americans simply represented four more targets to them. But Olson and his three troops were hardened by years of training for combat. They had put in their "dirt time"—shot countless rounds in all sorts of environments. They were masters of their game and knew how to push the envelope when it came to risk. They understood where the edges were in terms of their skills, weapons, and tactics.

When you have a comfort level for risk like that, it is easier to find the physical courage to engage the "enemy" when a crisis hits.

This is not to say that these men didn't experience fear. That wouldn't be normal. Existential fear will always be present where there is a high risk of loss. Olson and the men had trained for high-risk situations of this sort and were able to operate effectively with a pickup team in an ad hoc situation. Though they hadn't worked together as a team before, they all shared a common background, training, purpose, and ethos. This sharing of experience and purpose is seen in the seventh commitment of alignment—and demonstrates how each commitment in this book reinforces the others. Alignment allowed the team to move beyond physical courage to activate moral and spiritual strength. When the moment came for decisive action, they were able to enter the fight without hesitation. They didn't know if they were going to survive, but they did know that they were going to give all they had to get their teammates out.

The four grabbed their battle kit and as many grenades, rockets, and ammo as they could carry. After a brief chat with the QRF leader, the four loaded into their hardened Humvee and left the protection of the compound.

The QRF stood and watched.

I'm sure you could have heard a pin drop.

I may be making this up, but I think the reaction force leadership team felt shamed. They had reacted from their first plateau survival shadow. Not that Olson was trying to shame them, but shamed they were—this is a big deal in their culture. They quickly overcame their inertia when they were shown a different way.

Action is the only way to eliminate doubt.

The QRF team mobilized to join the small special operations team in their bid to help the Rangers.

Courage is a commitment. It is often obscured by fear and the negative conditioning of self-preservation. To stare down that fear wolf, you and your team can:

1. **Develop an unusually high tolerance for risk,**

2. **Make training as close to reality as possible, and . . .**

3. **Align around a stand, a code of conduct, that invokes courage.**

PLAYING IT SAFE
CAN GET YOU KILLED

A t first Mogadishu seemed relatively stable. The warlord Aidid gave the impression that he was in control. But then he wasn't, and Somalia descended into chaos. Where have you seen that play out? Venezuela descends into chaos, then Syria, Iraq, Sudan, Afghanistan. What country is next? Which industries have disappeared overnight—and which will do so soon?

Massive volatility and uncertainty will continue for the foreseeable future—perhaps forever. The QRF team was paralyzed by the fear and uncertainty brought on by volatility. The Rangers were on patrol and then they're in the middle of a massive firefight. The Black Hawk pilots lifted off for a routine sortie, then are fighting for their lives in the middle of a city in chaos. Uncertainty of that magnitude will paralyze anyone not trained to tolerate a high degree of risk.

To mitigate uncertainty and overcome your subconscious fear of risk, you must train for it. Even if you don't operate in a high-risk environment, you can train yourself and your group to handle rapid change and the existential threats to your team and company. Call it what you want—crisis response, risk mitigation, or scenario-based training. In the chapter on resiliency, I will discuss my work with Shell Oil. The leadership at Shell is aware of the need to train for risk. They know from experience that the culture and bottom line will be negatively impacted if they don't. Risk training is standard operating procedure (SOP) on their rigs, and it happens daily. As a result, Shell is one of the most resilient companies in the world. The volatility and uncertainty won't go away, but Shell employees will respond in a controlled manner instead of in a negative way when the shit hits the fan.

There is a saying in the SOF community: "The more you sweat in peace, the less you bleed in war."

Preparing for high risk requires that you press the edges of your team's comfort zone. If you're going to have a major fuckup, my SEAL mentor William McRaven taught me that it is best to have it in training (you will read his story in the trust chapter). A protected fail-safe environment will give you and the team confidence and resourcefulness when the real-world crisis shows up—where things are breaking down rapidly. You won't freeze in fear but will be able to stand your ground to respond with courage.

Risk is ratcheted up every time you visit this type of training. This ratcheting frames your mindset to take on more and more risk without becoming reckless. You and the team are able to regulate your own stress and fear, giving you greater perspective and appreciation for what you have the capacity to deal with.

To take on a risky mission in the SEALs, we use the crawl-walk-run method to ratchet up risk tolerance. When we were learning to parachute jump, for instance, we started from a three-foot-high wooden table. We practiced the parachute landing fall on the ground, and then we jumped from the table over and over. Once we had mastered that, we moved on to a small 30-foot tower and then to a 200-foot tower, sort of like ziplining with a parachute. From there, it was a static-line jump from a height of a thousand feet. When we were proficient with that risk, after many more jumps, we proceeded to free-fall training. There we learned how to maintain situational awareness, stabilize our body, pull the rip cord at the right height, and deal with any malfunctions. And we repeated the crawl-walk-run for this entire phase. We didn't embark on the first high-risk free-fall jump out of a perfectly good airplane until after all that training. Eventually teams are able to free-fall jump at night with oxygen and full equipment load into enemy territory.

Ratcheting up risk tolerance one degree at a time is like putting a frog in a pot of warm water and then turning up the heat under the pan (a sad metaphor coming from a frogman). The brilliant tactic dramatically improves skills in volatile and uncertain situations. It cultivates the team's capacity for facing risky situations with courageous action. In other words, it will habituate behaviors and actions that appear courageous to others, but are now SOP to the team.

In order to be courageous, you must do courageous things.

GET REAL

The Greek philosopher Aristotle considered courage to be a core virtue to develop in a leader. In his book *Nicomachean Ethics* he explains that courage exists as a middle path between the extremes of fear and boldness. Being too fearful leads to cowardice, while fearlessness can make one rash.

The dance is to find that middle ground through trial and error—in a setting as close to the actual mission conditions as possible. That requires realism in your training. We are not looking to add risk only to cultivate risk tolerance, but also to train with as much realism as possible, simulating the conditions for failure.

With this method you will find the boundary between bravado and cowardice through practice—in a realistic environment— where you can make the thoughts and behaviors of courage habitual. You will stare down the wolf of fear though the practice, through failure, and because your team will expect you to grow. They will be watching you and helping out! They need you to be courageous and are rooting for you.

Aristotle says:

The courageous man withstands and fears those things
which it is necessary to fear and withstand and on account
of the right reason, and how and when it is necessary to fear
or withstand them, and likewise in the case of being bold.

Thus, individuals can be fearful and bold for the right reasons: they won't let fear paralyze them. At the right time and for the right reason, they will act with courage.

Training for risk realistically helps develop courage when the reasons are right to be courageous. You closely observe your personal, team, and system failure points, areas that could compromise the mission. Let's call these the critical nodes. During your high-risk training you build redundancies and quick responses for when these nodes are negatively impacted. This avoids cascading failure—a situation in which one break leads to another until the whole system is compromised.

In the parachuting example, there are several critical nodes. Clearly, contact with the ground is an important one. In that final moment, that last inch, if you don't flare properly, bend your knees, or execute a proper parachute landing fall (PLF) if falling over, you can break bones or worse. Never mind compromising the mission. However, this one is not the most critical node. The moment of chute deployment is an even more important one. Worst-case scenario, that thin canopy never opens or the parachute only partially deploys. What to do in that moment? Train for it relentlessly and build redundancy in.

Every critical node requires a contingency plan or action. If your team—no matter what the profession—is heading into volatility, they can reduce uncertainty and cowardice by having a plan for when things go wrong. Practice it to gain certainty and to habituate the courage muscle by upping the risk incrementally. Sweat more in peace.

Eric Olson later became a four-star admiral and the commander of the Special Operations Command, or SOCOM. In that role he was quoted as saying: "What you do and what you tolerate in your presence best demonstrates your standards."

"What you do" relates to demonstrating the standard yourself—leading by example. If Olson had ordered those other operatives to go out but didn't expose himself to the same risk, they would have gone, but with less enthusiasm. "Hey, go ahead, guys, you lead the charge, I'm sure the QRF will follow. I'll hold down the fort here." That doesn't work well in high-risk situations. SOF leaders know they have to lead by example by training and participating in risk alongside the troops. In order to inspire courage in both his men and the QRF, Olson knew that he had to have demonstrated, and again demonstrate, a standard for courageous behavior.

What you tolerate in your presence is important. Olson had no authority to order the QRF out; they were strategic partners, not his subordinates. But he did know from experience that people can be inspired to action through the actions of others. He set a new standard for them through the example of the small team. Had he not led through his own example, he would also have given a stamp of approval to the QRF's lack of engagement.

Because we have walked away from most universal standards in Western culture, everyone stands for what "feels" right as opposed to what is best. And what feels right is biased and informed by those internal plateau maps and shadows. Everyone reacts to others' biases without seeing or admitting their own.

You can see that not holding to an agreed-upon standard for courageous action has become an issue. Always doing what you want or what feels good in the moment is not courageous. It is more likely to be a fear-based conditioned reaction. Until we examine those deeply conditioned behaviors that lead to our reactionary thinking, we will lack true courage.

It may not be you as the leader who lacks the courage. I am confident that many of you reading this hold yourself to an extremely high standard, one requiring courageous behavior. But your team could be locked in fear. Do you know if they will stand the ground with you when the next crisis hits? Does the culture of legalism in your organization restrain bold action? Can you demonstrate the move forward, showing the team your standard, and know for sure that they will follow? Or will you end up surrendering to the new lower standard of the group like I did at CBC?

This is a tough one, right? Sometimes it's a matter of not wanting to make people feel less than comfortable, not wanting to rock the boat because the status quo is working "okay." Perhaps there are gender, age, and ethnicity considerations that worry you. Challenging the team to that new standard could be critiqued as biased or discriminatory, especially by your fourth plateau peeps.

This has led to a weakening of overall standards of excellence, making courageous behavior a challenge. In the SEALs, the risks are so high this issue is diminished, though not eliminated entirely. Communication through words and actions has to be brutally clear and honest. Clarity and honesty are hallmarks of elite teams, and courage is displayed by taking a stand through the team's actions.

I believe everyone has the potential for courageous behavior when they stare down the wolf of fear—regardless of age, race, gender, or sexual orientation—and everyone can tolerate unbelievable risk through realistic training and practice.

Building a culture of courage is not easy, but it is worth it.

Courage flows from the heart—so it makes sense that the courage wolf is said to reside there. I use the Japanese term *kokoro* in my business, SEALFIT, which can be translated as "merging heart and mind into your actions." It combines the concept of courage with the notion of fifth plateau wholeness in action. From that place, your actions flow from a deep awareness of who you really are and why you do what you do—because you have overcome negative conditioning.

When you consider the second part of the word *courage—age*—I suggest to you that we are in an age of heart. It's what Olson showed on that battlefield. You as a leader of leaders—and as a teammate—must lead with your heart and mind merged into your actions. Only then can you take a stand in a crisis and know that your team will mobilize alongside you.

TAKE A STAND

When you lead from the heart, you understand why something needs to be done at an emotional level. Emotions are why we do the hard things. Thinking precedes action but often prevents right action. Once the thinking is done, your heart and emotions, free of shadow, need to lead the way. Developing a stand requires that you first think through all the consequences of your decisions to all parties and to the environment. Those consequences likely include potential personal or professional risk—sometimes big-time failure. You appreciate that those consequences will have an impact not just on you as the leader but also on the team and the entire organization. As a result, knowing where you stand and committing to acting from the heart involve risk.

Olson and his team were clear about their stand and knew what needed to be done. They were able to link their vision to the mission and to the current situation, where the Rangers were pinned down. It wasn't just about the immediate mission, however. Those

In order to take a stand, you must make decisions from both the head and the heart. Only then will you act with courage, not cowardice or rashness. You must have a strong vision about what needs to be done, a definitive stance on why it needs to be done, and clarity about why you're the one that needs to do it. In addition, you must be aware of the consequences and be willing to accept them because the mission is that important to you.

Rangers were their teammates in extremis. If Olson hadn't had his code of conduct, not only would more have perished but also the entire Somali mission would likely have been even more of an abject failure. But he and his team had absolute clarity about what needed to happen and would have done it alone if necessary.

DISASTER BREW

The failure of my ability to form an elite team at CBC had a silver lining. It forced me to clarify my personal mission and to step into courage again. I had to risk it all by standing my ground.

After the relationship with my wife's family had devolved into a first plateau food fight, I stepped back to gain deeper clarity around my vision of what I wanted to do with my life after the SEALs. I mentioned earlier that I had brought in an investor to help me grow the business. He and I discussed options for expanding the business, which he was willing to finance. He had already dumped $200,000 into the project, and it was a testament to his faith in me that he was ready to put in a lot more. Then I revealed to him that when he first invested, I had acquiesced to my partners' demands that he not be allowed into the real estate partnership that owned the CBC property.

This was a surprise to him. He wasn't thrilled to learn that he had no security underlying his investment, and this disclosure caused him to pause his plans to invest more.

The situation got even more VUCA when my teammates enacted their plan to take control of the business through a proxy fight.

I was forced to take a stand.

I had put my personal reputation on the line with this investor and the other friends and with my family members who had backed me. I owed them every ounce of energy I had to get them a return on their investment. In my opinion, new investment capital for expansion provided the best chance for that to happen. But to move forward, I had to rectify the wrong that had been done with regard to the real estate partnership. With that clarity, I stared down my fear of confrontation and acted following my moral compass. I won the fight on moral grounds, but at great personal cost.

A good way to gain appreciation for what you stand for and what you'll tolerate in the presence of others is to observe closely what you and your teammates do when you are all pushed to the edge. When you realize you've crossed a hidden red line, you'll be able to identify the unspoken rules for why and how you need things to be.

This is your integrity revealing itself to you under pressure.

You just know you must take a stand—you have to take

courageous action. In my case, I organized a buyout for a very small gain for my own shares and most CBC investors—except my partners wouldn't include the new investor, for reasons they would not disclose. I felt this was a deal breaker, but he persuaded me to accept the deal and not worry about him. He was happy that I had done all I could to protect his interests.

So I sold my interest in CBC to my brothers-in-law for peanuts and got far, far away. I was walking away from my baby, my first successful business venture, now worth tens of millions of dollars. But, I had to take a stand and learned that strength of character and having no regrets are more valuable than the money. Though my reputation was temporarily tarnished by my partners' smear campaign, my integrity remained intact. I was empowered because I had learned to connect to my heart and to find courage to face a new kind of risk in the business world. This epic fail provided me insight into how building an elite business team would be more challenging than what I had experienced in the SEALs.

BOLDLY GOING WHERE NONE HAVE GONE BEFORE

I n May of 2019, I was invited to speak to the launch team at SpaceX, started by the brilliant and eccentric spacefaring entrepreneur Elon Musk.

When I think about SpaceX, courage immediately comes to mind. Elon and his team are elite operators by most measures. They are courageous, know how to navigate VUCA, and have developed an incredible tolerance for risk. They train and test realistically and relentlessly and are willing to see epic fails on their way to success.

SpaceX tests everything they build at every stage of development. However, in their early days, they experienced a 50 percent fail rate on their rockets. They would send one up and it would explode or crash—yet they would call that launch a success.

Larger companies would take hits that serious and retrench, go back to the drawing board. Not SpaceX. They *expect* to fail from the get-go. They know they have to learn how to do things differently and better, in order to have a prayer of meeting their mission. The challenges that they take on are ridiculously complex, but this just fuels their passion and drive. They have to accept unbelievable risk, train relentlessly, and improve by testing and failing forward faster and faster until they nail it. Then they move on to the next target. They have mastered the military tool for handling VUCA, the *OODA loop.*

OODA looping is how elite teams find their way in complex situations. This acronym stands for observe, orient, decide, and act. I have written in detail about this concept in my book *The Way of the SEAL.* SpaceX utilizes it by performing a test and then observing and measuring what happens to all systems. They will then orient to the new reality that the data reveals. Then comes a new set of decisions. Finally they take courageous action. They don't need a perfect plan and don't wait for perfect conditions to execute. Then they repeat the process again and again. If there is a system or mission failure, they observe and orient themselves to the new data of what went wrong, create a new set of decisions, and take action again. Rinse and repeat. The OODA loop allows them to constantly speed up their process improvement and execution skills. The learning accelerates, while the failure rate decelerates. That's a winning combination.

Does that mean they control all their risk? Absolutely not.

In fact, the OODA loop allows them to work with even more elevated risk, knowing they have little control over the risk, only their response to it. Up until May of 2019, they'd been launching hunks of metal up into space, but now they intended to perform their first human space flight. And sending humans involves an entirely new level of risk, one that makes many of the engineers and scientists very nervous. Their fear wolves were howling. But I know that they have trained their risk tolerance and have the courage to send real humans into space.

They have taken a stand and developed a "failure is not an option" mindset.

Many misunderstand that saying. To me it means that we embrace failure as we find our way to success. When knocked down seven times, you will get up eight, and stronger. It doesn't mean you can't tolerate failure. That is how the SpaceX team sees it, too. But that doesn't mean that they don't have negative conditioning that could cripple their leader's decision-making. That is why they are adamant about personal and team development. It is why they invited me to speak to the team.

The elite wilderness firefighter smokejumper's code applies to this team of rocket men and women: "We do today what others won't, so we can do tomorrow what others can't."

As I write this, no government or private company can send a manned spaceship to another planet, let alone to colonize it. That, however, is SpaceX's mission—to make the human species a spacefaring, multi-planetary species, starting with Mars. Elon said he would like to die on Mars, *just not on impact.* By the time this book is published, the team should already be working on their first manned space flight—there's no going back. They have thrown their hearts into the action because their stand and vision are set to change the course of humanity.

I mentioned that I was asked to speak to the launch team because they were scared and willing to admit it. They were being human, not acting like bureaucratic robots. They wanted me to teach them mental toughness and emotional coping skills, which they knew I did for elite teams. It is easier for the astronauts to face the mission with courage than the engineers. The astronauts are like Navy SEALS: they have trained relentlessly since their early twenties in extraordinarily realistic and high-risk environments. This is their next grand adventure and they understand the stakes, as well as the consequences of failure. That is how I would view it. The astronauts have ratcheted up their risk tolerance throughout their career.

However, the engineers who have developed the technology and the launch team who sends the rockets into space are not trained like that. This is a defining moment where failure would have dire consequences to others' lives and their own reputations. While the risk for this part of the team isn't to their life, they feel it almost as acutely as the astronauts. How are they going to deal with that as a team?

We talked about how to learn to control what they can control, and how to train their mindset and emotional capacity to manage this new stress, the way special operators do. I feel honored to have the opportunity to work with this fifth plateau team.

Courage is the first commitment. The one thing that can destroy courageous behavior in a heartbeat is a breakdown of trust.

In the next chapter, we'll discuss the second commitment: how to build that trust.

SDTW Exercise 2:
WHAT DO YOU STAND FOR?

Perform the same preparatory drill as in the first exercise to clear your mind and to access your heart. Now contemplate and answer the following questions:

1. What am I attached to that causes me to avoid risk and the consequences of failure? (for example, my reputation, my job, the appearance of being in control, my physical safety, etc.)

2. Do I train for risk at all?

3. Do I train for risk realistically, relentlessly, and continuously?

4. Is what I stand for what everyone else stands for, or do I stand for an uncommon level of excellence, of personal risk, of courage?

5. Create a statement of your stand, articulated in no more than five bullets. (Examples of possible points include "I stand for freedom, leaving nobody behind, being a courageous leader, self-mastery in service to my team and mission.")

LEADERSHIP
COMMITMENT
#2

COMMIT TO
TRUST

STARE DOWN THE FEAR OF FAILURE

Commander William McRaven was my SEAL Team Three commanding officer. He had come to the team after receiving a master's degree from the Naval Postgraduate School. Prior to Monterey, he was with the unit formerly known as SEAL Team Six.

When he arrived at Team Three, I dusted off my copy of

The Theory of Special Operations. This was McRaven's treatise that came out of his master's research, which quickly became a must-read for SEAL leaders. He studied a number of special operations missions from World War II through modern-day Israeli special forces, and distilled a theory that all successful operations have a few things in common. These were a rabid focus on simplicity, solid operational security, repetition in preparation, the element of surprise, speed of action, and clarity of purpose—good things for any leader of an elite team to consider. McRaven already had a reputation as a highly intelligent man. In fact, many considered him one of the smartest leaders in the SEALs. His career was on the rebound after he had questioned his former team's culture as unprofessional, perhaps even reckless. That team's commander was a barefisted brawler type who found joy in slithering, knife in mouth, onto an enemy beach. McRaven was competent at that, and also at crafting and pitching future warfighting concepts. It is plausible that the team's commander viewed him more as a manager than as a leader of hard-core SEALs. In my opinion he was wrong, but McRaven got fired anyhow for not aligning with that culture. Though his career was not looking good, instead of taking this defeat lying down, McRaven literally wrote the book on special ops mission success.

I was fortunate to observe up close and personal his leadership at SEAL Team Three and later at Naval Special Warfare Group One. When I first met him, I was just coming off a deployment and taking over the leadership of another platoon. Before I tell you more about how he built and rebuilt trust at the team, let me revisit my fear wolf and see how it tripped me up in front of McRaven.

Always radically mission focused, I was inclined to work hard, learn and train my ass off. But when I got back after months of training or from a long deployment, I would also blow off steam by partying hard with my enlisted teammates. I was taking a risk because doing so as an officer was frowned upon, though up to this point it hadn't been a problem. During my second deployment with SEAL Team Three I had some intense missions followed by foreign port visits, where my team and I enjoyed the local fare. By the end of my six-month deployment, I felt pushed to the brink by the combination of the intense performance pressure and excessive partying. I was burning the candle at both ends and could sense that something was about to give.

One fear wolf shadow of mine back then was the tendency to use alcohol to celebrate, as if I earned it and deserved it. I relied on it to feel alive and also to avoid feeling incomplete. Of course I didn't know any of that then. What was I avoiding? Though my higher self knew that I was enough and didn't need more alcohol, I ignored that voice and kept going. That pattern was deeply subconscious, with an unhealthy relationship to alcohol part of my family's shadow for generations on both sides.

Sure enough, about a month after that deployment ended, and a couple of months into McRaven's tenure at SEAL Team Three, the gasket blew. I was out with the boys after a training mission, overdid it, and got into some minor trouble with a local. Faced with a narrow range of options and not knowing me from Adam, McRaven fired me. While he didn't remove me from SEAL Team Three, he removed me from my platoon and put me in the operations shop. This was huge blow to my ego. I went from the number one ranked lieutenant to canned in one day. And though many in the command went to bat for me, telling the CO he had over-reacted and lobbying to reinstate me, McRaven wasn't moved. I sadly watched Lieutenant Hart, not his real name, take over my platoon.

I was very close to my teammates and felt I had really let them down. I considered leaving the Navy, but had a year left on my com-mitment. So I hunkered down and got back to work. The platoon grudgingly accepted their new leader. He was a good guy and turned out to be effective—though with a very different style than mine. My screw-up caused me a lot of regret, but it also forced me to stare down that fear wolf issue, providing a crucial growth opportunity. In fact, within nine months, I had moved from the achiever to the equalizer perspectives (referring to the Five Plateaus introduced earlier). I had stopped chasing thrills and girls, gotten married, started therapy, and recommitted to practicing Zen. I began to look within for measures of my success. Back on my meditation bench, and humbled by the failure, my leadership style became more authentic.

Let me get back to the first part of the story.

A few months went by while I toiled in the operations shop as-sisting with team logistics and planning. My old platoon, Alpha, was preparing for their pre-deployment test up the coast in Morro Bay.

This was to be their operational readiness exam before deploying overseas. The op was to prove that the platoon was prepared for combat, and McRaven needed to pay close attention to validate firsthand that they were ready. But he was not going to get in the way of his training cadre or the platoon leadership, so he stayed on-shore while the platoon was at sea.

The team got to Morro Bay in a fishing craft to blend in with the locals. The plan was to launch their zodiac boats for an over-the-beach insertion. Two swimmer scouts were to reconnoiter the surf zone and a beach landing site for the boats. Then they would take the boats through the surf and across the beach. From there, the task was to perform a raid to destroy a missile launch facility.

SEALs are fond of saying, "The only easy day was yesterday."

Which proved to be true once again.

Morro Bay is renowned for its unpredictable and heavy surf conditions during the winter. The waves can be innocuous along the shoreline, but at the bay's entrance they get funneled into boomers that can reach up to fifty feet. The Coast Guard has a station near Morro Bay, and it is where they do their heavy surf passage training. The night of that op, King Neptune was raging at Morro Bay. It was definitely no place for small boats with commandos to be coming ashore—but hey, that's what SEALs do.

The team got to their insert point around midnight and launched the boats. The seas were gut-wrenchingly shitty and unwelcoming. The lieutenant sent his two swimmer scouts, nicknamed Johnny Utah and Dublin, into the choppy, wet darkness.

These men were phenomenal swimmers and extremely

competent warriors. They made their way to the outer edge of the surf, sensing whether it was suitable to bring the boats through. If so, they would proceed to find a target landing site for the team. They would then signal from the beach for the boats to come in.

They never made it through the surf zone.

Instead, they had a "holy shit" moment. It was clear these waves would toss their boats and potentially kill someone. They turned back to the waiting team and warned the lieutenant that this was a no-go. Lietenant Hart, the team leader, was a very good swimmer and surfer and wanted badly to go in, but he had to trust the judgment of his teammates. In a real-world scenario, he would likely make that call alone. In this training exercise he decided to head back to the support vessel and check in with Team Three's second-in-command, the executive officer (XO). After he and the XO went back and forth, they agreed to call off the op and return to the forward operating base (FOB). They would wait to see if conditions improved the next day.

One of the lieutenant's fear wolf issues was to be a pleaser. He really looked up to McRaven and did not want to let him down. He felt like this call to abort the mission was doing just that. It was not the wrong call, and he was supported by the XO, but he still wondered if he had wimped out. He felt he had failed and later questioned whether he could have found another way to get the op done—without taking the boats in. So focused had he and the others been on their original plan that there had been no discussion of other courses of action to get the mission accomplished. The team leader may have been blinded by the bias of his own planning. The fear wolf is always lurking around risk, waiting to nip courageous action on the ankle.

The next day McRaven did indeed question the decision and the lack of consideration for alternative plans. He gave the lieutenant the impression he could have worked the problem through some more before throwing in the towel. After all, SEALs are supposed to be able to operate in the most severe maritime environments. SEAL Team Three needed to learn the limits of their operators, boats, and drivers in those sea states.

At any rate, the surf was just as brutal that next day, and when McRaven asked the team to take another go at the op, the captain of the fishing vessel refused to go. This put the nail in the coffin of this ill-fated mission. The team packed up and went home. The exam was still deemed a "pass" for the quality of planning, and the valuable lessons learned. Alpha Platoon deployed on their overseas mission shortly after.

Months later the surf was up again in Morro Bay and another platoon, Echo, was preparing for their own operational readiness exam. This event offered McRaven a inadvertent chance for a do-over of the first disappointing Morro Bay experience. He went to check in with Echo Platoon—to see their plan and observe the training. He saw that a Naval Special Warfare Special Boat unit was there to support the platoon. These units had evolved from the fabled riverine units that supported SEALs in Vietnam's Mekong Delta. That particular boat unit was led by a SEAL officer, my former teammate in Alpha Platoon. That hard charger also wanted to test the limits of his boats and crew in the heavy surf conditions. This time they would attack the surf with the sturdy Rigid Hull Inflatable Boat (RHIB).

ELEMENTS OF TRUST

There are the three elements of trust that I would like to address, which McRaven demonstrated through this series of incidents. They are *transparency, humility,* and *follow-through*. Let's finish the story before we look at them in more detail.

RHIBs are 30-foot-long high-speed boats with hard hulls and rubber inflatable buoyancy tubes on the outside. They have massive engines and external water jets for propulsion and can carry a squad of armed-up operators along with the boat's crew of four—all told, eleven or twelve operators. McRaven was observing the SEALs run rehearsals for their mission when he noticed two RHIBs loitering inside the bay. He took a Zodiac out to see how they were doing, wondering if they were going to make a run at the surf. It just so happened that the surf that day was roughly the same as it was when Hart's team got turned back. The young SEAL officer and the boat's crew chief told McRaven that they were confident they could make it through the surf. McRaven wasn't convinced, so he asked again and the officer said that they had trained for this in Alaska, and that his crews were the best they had. All aboard agreed. They were going.

"Grab me a life vest, because I'm coming with you," said McRaven.

In a moment he was strapped in and the boats turned toward the surf. Getting through surf that big is all about timing. The drivers needed to wait for the set to run through. This particular set had three boomers, then a short lull before the next set rolled in. The three waves came and went, and McRaven braced for the acceleration. But the boat didn't move—the driver waited for just a moment longer. Then he hit the gas and the boat's engines roared back to life, the RHIB heading up, up, and over the first massive wave, exposing its jet thrusters to open air. It crested the top and hung suspended for several seconds before crashing down in the trough between the first and second wave. The operator in the front of the boat was ejected into the ocean, and the boat stalled in its tracks. The driver gunned toward the second wave as shouts of "Man overboard!" rang out. They had no choice, though, and the same scenario started to play out. They went airborne for a full five seconds—it must have felt like a lifetime—before slamming down and this time breaking the hull. The third wave didn't stop for them. It picked the boat up and turned it on its head.

The RHIB and all passengers tumbled end over end and came to rest upside down, with the massive waves continuing to plunge over the hapless crew. McRaven and another officer almost drowned, and four others went to the hospital with broken bones and lacerations. It was a serious disaster—but it could have been much worse.

The training exercise turned rescue operation saw all able-bodied operators aiding in the recovery. The SEAL platoon was quick to get a Zodiac out to recover Commander McRaven, while the second RHIB recovered the others. In short order they were back on the beach, glad that everyone was still alive. Too often in the SOF VUCA world these missions have the worst imaginable consequences, so when everyone was deemed to be okay, it was considered a blessing.

Back at SEAL Team Three the formal investigation began. I was not alone in wondering if the boat unit leader and my new CO would take a career body blow for this one.

Not so.

McRaven was the senior officer on the scene, and there was no way that those above him in his chain of command would be out of line to question his decision to allow the boats to go through the surf—not to mention his decision to risk his life to go with them. McRaven needed to be absolutely transparent and to own his role in the situation. He owned the consequences just because he had been there, which was his burden of leadership.

The investigation ended up clearing him, and actually supported McRaven for not shying from risk. The SEALs needed to continue to push the envelope to discover their capabilities and boundaries. Shying from risk would get more people killed or compromise the mission in combat. The loss of a $500,000 boat was a small price to pay.

I soon saw how McRaven extracted learning from everything he did. He did not want the command to engage in second-guessing or risk-averse thinking as the result of accidents like this. With his guidance, the team would improve on their risk mitigation and training for high-risk operations. The incident informed his thinking on how SEALs could get through tough surf conditions in enemy territory—which led in turn to innovations such as employing stealth Jet Skis.

Most important, the incident was a contributing factor in the creation of the outstanding special warfare small boat training that came a few years later. At the time of the SEAL Team Three incident, the SEALs did not have dedicated selection training for its small boat operators. SEALs drove their own Zodiac boats and the Special Boat Units would provide drivers when supporting with their RHIBs or riverine boats. A new training detachment was started at BUD/S for the specialized training of what are now called Special Warfare Combatant-Craft Crewman, or SWCC. Those who make it through the training are masters of their crafts—experts at navigating and reading the ocean, operating the boats in high-risk enemy territory, and delivering SEALs to their maritime targets.

McRaven was utterly transparent and truthful with the investigation itself. He didn't cast blame on the boat officer in charge; McRaven owned his part and didn't try to mitigate the responsibility that his presence as a senior officer brought with it. He didn't say things like "Well, I just wanted to see how the crews would operate. I was not interfering with their training mission." Many leaders would have let their fear wolf cover their ass. This one didn't. He owned it.

Transparency of the facts and ownership of the results, particularly with your fuckups, are crucial in developing trust. Conversely, *denying* ownership and responsibility and failing to be transparent are the fastest ways to destroy trust.

Then there was the follow-through.

McRaven followed through to ensure everyone was going to recover and get back operational as soon as possible. Also, he checked that any family needs were sorted out. Then he had the team examine how they could improve risk management for these types of operations. Whatever he said he was going to do, in all the instances that I observed, he did it. He was relentless with follow-through.

The last thing you want from a high-performing team is to ease up on the throttle after a screw-up. But that is a common reaction in the corporate world. At the same time, you don't want the team to press on without slowing down just enough to learn from the situation, either. The pace of operations is relentless for the SEALs, as it is for every business. It would have been easy to let this incident slip into the rearview mirror without the requisite learning.

McRaven did find the time to pause and learn. He balanced the team precisely between cowardice and rashness in the manner that Aristotle talked about. The team was encouraged to tolerate and learn from risk, but not to shirk it, even when things don't go according to plan. He built great trust in his leadership. While at SEAL Team Three and beyond, he continued to support high-risk training evolutions, remained personally involved, and learned from the mistakes. His ownership of the Morro Bay incident didn't diminish his appetite for risk, which was hugely important for the team to see.

Failures due to acceptable risk were not to be taken as personal failings, nor would they be allowed to degrade the standards of the team.

Too many leaders fear the transparency of personal failures, hiding behind convenience and the comfort of silence or inaction. Stare down your fear wolf and admit your mistakes immediately, and don't say you're going to do something unless you have every intention of following through. If for some reason you can't get that thing done, then you'd better have a damned good reason why and communicate it clearly. Be true to your word and maintain a relentless standard for transparency.

HUMBLE PIE

Humility is forged through risking, failing, and learning, as with the Morro Bay incident. This humility is best cultivated through training, rather than waiting for a real-world incident to smack you down. I recommend you allow your teams to screw up and to cultivate humility by risking those very screw-ups. Humility comes when you stop pretending to be perfect, better, smarter, or more competent than others. Do not fear failure, as it is your best chance to grow. In the SEALs, someone can die in a risky training operation just as they can in combat. It is a necessary risk. Your risk level may be lower, but the point is that by making mistakes in training, you lessen the chance they will be made in real-life scenarios, leading to better results.

This incident was just one of many risk learning moments for McRaven. He used these to examine his own patterns of decision-making, growing to be a more authentic leader as a result.

He didn't pretend to be perfect, smarter, or more competent than others in the command or outside of it. In the eyes of the team, risking failure and being humble when it happened made him more human. That is what authenticity looks like—being real and able to connect to the average teammate—authenticity breeds trust. The team saw that this leader didn't expect everyone else to take on the risk except for him. Also, he didn't keep them from learning and growing by avoiding institutional risk, which could have had a negative impact on their careers.

Notice I have not used the word *vulnerable* to describe Olson or McRaven. The concept of vulnerability has been made popular by the talented author Brené Brown. This has become a buzzword in corporate training as of late. But telling SEALs or any military operators to be vulnerable is like advising them to expose their back to the enemy. It makes far more sense to me that leaders be authentic— open to being wrong, open to other people's ideas and perspectives, and courageous in connecting to their heart and connecting at a heart level with their teammates.

This could just be semantics, but in my view, to be vulnerable means to be open to attack, which decreases trust when others sense that. Warriors and leaders today need to close those openings to attack while opening their hearts to make better decisions. That doesn't mean that the cloak falls off emotionally—it means that their weaknesses are closed off to exploitation.

For instance, I mentioned earlier that one of my conditioned vulnerabilities is codependence, bred into me by my family in formative years. This opened me to be exploited easily by narcissists and borderline personalities, who somehow sense this vulnerability a mile away. So I have worked to close that opening, which has allowed me to be more authentic about who I am, including my many imperfections. Similarly, McRaven wasn't vulnerable with his men, but he was authentic. With your immediate team, the people with whom you work directly, you have to open your heart for a deeper understanding and connection.

That all takes courage, and it develops great trust.

TRANSPARENCY

Each of the three elements of trust—transparency, follow-through, and humility—have behavioral practices that will further develop the skill.

When we are talking about transparency, it is critical that you check your ego at the door. You must not pretend to your team that you have all of the answers. Be willing to immediately admit your mistakes and air your dirty laundry with your team, because they will see it anyway—they're always watching. If you try to hide your flaws or pretend that you're perfect in spite of them, then you lose credibility. Develop a practice of airing your dirty laundry. Having a formal debrief process is very useful for this.

Often, when leaders screw up, they lose courage. They will identify themselves with their mistakes, bringing the entire team down as a result. Don't identify with your mistakes. Let go of any attachment to desired outcomes and quickly move on from mistakes that preclude those outcomes. Admit that you're not perfect and that you're going to screw up. And when you do, embrace the suck and learn from it—and then again move on. Many of the expectations, outcomes, and mistakes that I have let go of have claw marks on them, but at least I am not holding on to them anymore. That includes my screw-up at SEAL Team Three. Authentic leaders readily admit their mistakes and easily let go of regrets.

FOLLOW-THROUGH

An elite leader and an elite team will be relentless with follow-through.

A typical leader's day is comprised of hundreds of small, seemingly inconsequential decisions, commitments, and offers—and a few big ones. It's easy to think of those small things as not important. We can get it in our heads that we've handled the big things well, so we are good to go. And we're too important to spend much energy on the small things anyway. We often say yes to too many things and then regret our commitments, choosing not to do some of them right now—or ever. Blowing off the small things and not following up on commitments in a timely manner will erode trust.

While you might have one big task or project that you're focused on completing, you can blow it altogether in the trust department if you don't follow through on the various little things you also committed to. The devil really is in the details—those seemingly inconsequential decisions and commitments you make. The big wins come by accumulating many small wins with relentless follow-through. The big fails come from forgetting, ignoring, or just not following through on the small commitments because you are too busy or impatient to give them your full attention.

Develop the muscle of committing only to the most important actions, and then follow through relentlessly.

HUMILITY

As stated above, you can practice humility by being *willing* to mess up. Always try something new that you know is going to be hard or do something you know well but push yourself harder than you did the last time. Just one degree more difficult is sufficient, keeping you always emptying your ego cup as you step into that new territory. Humility means risking failure, being okay when it happens, and not taking it personally. In this way, humility and transparency are close cousins; both cultivate authenticity.

By the way, it is no news flash that opening your heart to your team is difficult for men to do. Not being able to do so actually makes men vulnerable—that inability to connect is itself a weakness. Remember that to be authentic, you must close the openings of your weaknesses. You do that by training your heart to connect deeply to your teammates—to experience more mutual trust and understanding.

I believe humility must be a daily practice. A concrete example of this is to give credit to others, even for your successes. When the team wins, even if you're largely responsible for the outcome, always give credit to the team. McRaven was especially skilled at this, and it served him well. It didn't feel like a leadership tactic, though; he meant what he said. You can also practice by distancing yourself from "I" statements and begin using "we" statements instead. In our Unbeatable Mind training, this is called taking your eyes off yourself and putting them on your team. And when things go bad, take responsibility, even if it wasn't your fault.

Humility is also deepened through a daily practice of controlled breathing and meditation. I recommend you implement this as a daily practice—ideally with your team. I have been teaching these valuable skills to SEALs and other clients since 2007, and have seen their humbling impact firsthand. The reason is that they help you to disengage from your ego-driven stories. You will connect to your spiritual center, which is pure humility.

BOX BREATHING

This breathing practice simply involves controlling the pace of your breathing by taking slow, deep diaphramatic breaths, and then holding the breath after each inhale and exhale. When done daily it will reduce your stress, help you maintain focus, deepen your concentration power, and elevate your overall performance in all areas of your life. I recommend twenty minutes first thing in the morning.

1. Sit upright in a chair or on your meditation bench or cushion, and slowly exhale through your mouth.

2. Slowly and deeply inhale through your nose to a count of four or five. Relax your belly, using your diaphragm and all the muscles meant for breathing. Feel the air fill your lungs all the way, but don't overdo it.

3. Hold your breath after the inhale for a count of four or five. Try not to create any downward pressure while holding the breath. It should feel light, as if you are still inhaling.

4. Exhale through your nose for a count of four or five, expelling all the air from your lungs and pressing your belly button toward your spine.

5. Hold your breath again after the exhale for a count of four or five. Repeat this for the time you have committed.

This can become a stacked practice for arousal control (stress management) and attention control (concentration). When you are practicing, keep your attention on the breath pattern. You can do this with an internal count or by visualizing the numbers or box pattern. Then when you notice that your mind has wandered off that object of concentration (which it will), you direct it back to the object. Over time you will develop greater staying power on the object, and less distractibility. The practice of sitting there, closing your eyes, and breathing together as a team is a special experience—something most people find to be awkwardly uncomfortable at first. It will develop a great deal of intimacy and humility quickly though. Teams that breathe and meditate together will have greater trust in one another. Trust me on this—this practice alone has transformed the performance and depth of connection of my own teams.

It is important to learn how to skillfully use the breathing and meditation tools. They are meant to evolve your character—to be a more peaceful, connected, whole, intuitive, and insightful. If you employ these tools improperly, you can find yourself obsessing about certain negative or fantastical thought patterns. Further, you could mistake a peak experience for real change, or worse, imprint a negative psychological pattern deeper.

In short, there are a lot of potholes if the training isn't taught skillfully. One of my meditation teachers liked to say, "If you're an asshole and you meditate for thirty years, you're likely to be a more focused asshole."

So when you begin your meditation practice, both by yourself and with your team, try not to lose sight of the fact that the type of practice is as important as how you practice. First understand *why* you want to do the work, such as to evolve your character of authenticity and emotional depth, and *what* tools are appropriate. Utilize meditative practices for self-awareness and improvement and to foster greater humility—not to become more financially successful or to turn into a more focused jerk. Box breathing is an excellent starting point, and our Unbeatable Mind training (www.unbeatablemind.com) could be a resource.

TRUST AT HARVARD YARD

I had the unique opportunity to visit with and speak to the physicians at the Harvard Medical School Department of Neurosurgery, thanks to my student Rodolfo Alcedo Guardia, MD.

Dr. Alcedo Guardia had discovered my training system some time ago, and in 2016 attended a SEALFIT event called the 20X. The name is a reference to our belief that you can train yourself to achieve twenty times more than you think you can. The event is twelve hours of nonstop intense physical, mental, and emotional team training. The main idea is to force the teams to open up to their hearts to learn how to develop greater trust and courage.

In May of 2017, he invited me to Harvard to speak to the surgeons and professors in the Department of Neurosurgery. While there, I was allowed to observe their grand rounds, where once a week they would peer-review their most difficult cases. This was a no-holds-barred discussion, full disclosure of the good, bad, and the ugly of the cases discussed. The presenter was selected because he or she had led a recent surgery that was not only difficult, but where the decisions could be challenged. In other words, the doctor might have dropped the ball.

It was clear to me that the team was uncertain if the doctor that I observed had made the right call concerning a patient's care. The presenting surgeon was on the hot seat, and they were grilling her, but she was not taking anything personally. I was immediately reminded of our SEAL debriefs, which had the same qualities. The whole exercise was fascinating, definitely an elite team in action.

Here were individuals at the top of their field, engaged in saving lives while exhibiting complete transparency in their decisions at great personal risk. They were practicing humility and hid nothing from one another, at least in my observation.

It would not have made sense to do so. The risks were too great, from the standpoint of patient care and on the basis of liability and financial considerations. As a team, they had to put everything on the table and get *brutally* honest feedback so that everyone could learn and grow from the experience. The communication style was quite matter-of-fact. No one was defensive about the decisions that had been made. The presentation was open and clear and the doctor was able to respond to penetrating questions, all in the spirit of learning and improvement.

That level of transparency was the underpinning of the trust they all had for each other.

When it came to humility, Dr. Alcedo Guardia is himself a model citizen. He was and is passionate about improving himself. That's what brought him to stare down his fear wolf at the 20X training. He's all about service, and the last time I checked in with him, he was working in Puerto Rico to provide medical services after most of the doctors left due to a recent hurricane. Where once he spent 20 percent of his time working in Puerto Rico with the remaining time at Harvard, he's now reversed that allocation of time. His people needed him, and he was willing to subjugate his own needs to support them.

Another physician I met at Harvard was the department head, Dr. Mohammad Ali Aziz-Sultan. This gentleman spent several hours with me during his busiest time of day. Dr. Aziz-Sultan is one of the most interesting and humble individuals I've ever had the pleasure of meeting. It was clear that humility starts at the top at Harvard.

Dr. Aziz-Sultan is an Afghan refugee who escaped his home country when the mujahideen ran the roost. He ended up in Europe penniless, then made his way to Canada and eventually the United States. He found the means to pay his way through college and medical school and was hired by Harvard University in 2013. During our conversation, he said to me, "Mark, we're at the top of our game here. We make a lot of money and have a terrific amount of prestige. But we're all tapped out. We're giving all we've got."

The team often performs surgeries of ten to twelve hours in duration, requiring intense focus. They can log twelve-to-fourteen-hour days for weeks on end. They are not alone in that many high-performance teams, such as SEALs, astronauts, and neurosurgeons, must learn how to handle the negative impact of sleep deprivation and stress. Dr. Aziz-Sultan had the humility to ask me how they could all find more balance and energy to be more effective in their work. Similar to the SpaceX team, Dr. Aziz-Sultan and his leaders believed that they could always learn something new, and they weren't afraid to ask for help. They didn't believe that because they were the best in their field they had everything figured out.

Their follow-through as a team was as elite as anyone can imagine—the attention to detail stunning. The surgical procedures themselves, the preparation, the follow-up with the patient, and the learning—all of these require commitment to doing exactly what they said they will do, or quite literally, people can die.

The Harvard surgeons stare down the wolf as a team, dealing with any negative conditioning that could hold them back or lead to a casualty. They demonstrated a great deal of trust in one another, and also in themselves and in their skills—not from some egotistical sense of being better than others, but from the humility, transparency, and follow-through to which they commit on a daily basis.

FAILURE OF TRANSPARENCY

After I finally walked away from the Coronado Brewing Company, I had a few years where I tried a number of different start-ups—and I was incrementally more successful each time. In one, I was a hired gun serving as interim CEO. That went well, until the venture capitalists involved brought in a "more qualified" CEO, who soon ran the company out of money. Afterward, I started a sole proprietor consultancy to advise other start-up entrepreneurs. During this time, I was also hired as adjunct professor of leadership at the University of San Diego while I labored toward a PhD there. I was clearly seeking my muse, looking to find a solid foothold in my post-active-duty SEAL life. But it was my next venture that fed my fear wolf another juicy morsel and taught me about just how ephemeral trust can be.

Two SEAL teammates had started a training business called Arena Adventures, and they asked me to be the CEO. Arena wanted to bring experiential team building with an outdoor adventure theme to companies. I did a few events with them to get a sense of what the business was all about and then decided to join up.

Fast forward three months, to a point where we were ready to expand the team to meet our mission. We had identified two experts in adventure leadership training who had skills we felt important, skills that couldn't easily be contracted out. We decided to bring them on to the team with an equity position. I hoped that the addition of these two would create a more balanced and experienced team.

About a month after they were brought on, the two newcomers came to me privately and told me that they were having difficulty handling the personality of one of the cofounders. It was an "us versus him" speech, and they wanted him off the team. Because I was the CEO, they maintained, it was my job to make it happen. My brain was saying, "Why don't you guys talk to him yourselves?" but my fear wolf, not wanting to rock the boat, pushed me into halfheartedly agreeing. I felt really awkward in that meeting, because, well, it was awkward! I wasn't ready to let anyone go, either.

So I did nothing.

I was obviously not transparent to the cofounders with this situation; the uncertainty and complexity were exactly *why* I wasn't being transparent about it. I had not yet developed the emotional courage that I am preaching in these pages. So I breached the commitment of trust by not being transparent until it was too late. Things like this stay secret only so long—the truth will always find the light of day. Word eventually got back to the cofounder that the three of us had met in secret to discuss his removal. The situation exploded, as you would expect it to.

The need to be utterly transparent was not transparent to me then.

It is now.

To try to salvage things, I told him that I had screwed up and that I should have come to him right away. Then I stepped down from my position. I could see in hindsight that I had the gut feeling that the situation wasn't right and that I needed to do something about it, but I didn't. The denied transparency made a bad situation worse. I should have aired the dirty laundry and checked my ego to resolve the situation right away. Not doing so destroyed the trust the team had for me and for one another. At that point, resigning was the right action. The business never got off the ground after that, and all of them went on to other adventures.

GREASE THE WHEELS

Three months after relieving me of my platoon leadership, McRaven gave me a second chance. He offered me leadership of a new platoon heading to the Middle East, along with Arabic language training. He also offered to help clean up any service record issues so I could be promoted to lieutenant commander (which I was, retiring fifteen years later as a full commander). He admitted that in hindsight, the facts of the situation had been grossly overblown and that he had overreacted. He wanted to make it right, but I had already accepted new orders to the SEAL Delivery Vehicle (SDV) team in Hawaii—and my soon-to-be wife Sandy was excited to go. So I passed on the offer, though I greatly appreciated this gesture.

Trust is like the glue filling in and firming support around the team. They can then operate without being concerned about betrayal, withheld support, or recriminations when something goes wrong.

If trust is the glue, then respect is the lubricant that takes the squeak out of imperfect communication and interactions. Things just run more smoothly when there is respect.

In the next chapter, we'll talk about how to build and maintain the commitment of respect.

SDTW Exercise 3:
TRANSPARENCY, HUMILITY, AND FOLLOW-THROUGH

You know the drill—prepare your mind to get really honest with yourself and your team. Then meditate on and contemplate the following:

1. Are you withholding important information from your team or a teammate?

2. When was the last time you were completely transparent with your team?

3. Have you taken full responsibility for your screw-ups, or have you left some on the floor for others to trip over?

4. Do you consider yourself humble? If so, what do you do daily to cultivate humility?

5. Do you relentlessly follow through on your commitments—even the small ones?

6. What or who are you blowing off right now? Commit to pay attention to the details while moving relentlessly forward on the big initiatives.

LEADERSHIP COMMITMENT
#3

COMMIT TO
RESPECT

STARE DOWN THE FEAR OF JUDGMENT

The aphorisms of the **SEALS** are legendary and many. These sayings were how we passed down learning and created culture well before our actual ethos was written down. One that I particularly enjoyed was this: "In case of war, break glass."

Associated with that phrase was a picture of a frog inside a glass jar, decked out with a loaded ammo bandolier, web gear, grenades, and automatic weapons. SEALs are also known as frogmen, or just frogs, a nod to our Underwater Demolition Team roots. The clear meaning is that the frogs are to be kept behind glass, locked up, until war breaks out. It was too dangerous to have them roaming the streets, threatening the locals (typically it was the local girls who had to be wary). SEALs are custom-built for war.

I first saw that image on a T-shirt while attending BUD/S training. I thought it was pretty cool, joking with some buddies that there might actually be SEALs locked up somewhere, waiting for the glass to break. I learned later that I wasn't far off. Indeed, there are some badass SEALs whom the head shed has broken the glass to send them on dark ops or for special assignments.

Like you would expect, the guys behind the glass are not chasing glory, fame, or fortune. They are the quiet professionals, the disciplined masters of their craft. And they set the bar for . . .

Respect.

Captain Jim O'Connell was the deputy (second-in-command) at the Naval Special Warfare Development Group (DEVGRU), the SEAL elite counterterrorist unit, when he decided to end his career at the top. On active duty for approximately twenty-four years, he had been deployed most of that time while his wife and family manned the home fort. The SEAL head shed tried hard to convince him to stay for the higher admiral "flag ranks," but he had promised his wife that since the first twenty-four years were about him and his career, the next twenty-four were for them both.

That worked just fine—until 9/11.

Suddenly it was not about him anymore. The country needed

him. The Navy canceled his retirement plans, and two years later, after the Iraq invasion, he was given command of the SEAL units prosecuting the war effort.

In case of war, break glass.

The Navy pulled O'Connell out of the jar and plopped him back in the hot seat because he was the best leader they had for that job. He was respected and apolitical, and he got results. He cared more about winning than about his reputation or career. As the new head of Naval Special Warfare Group One, he needed to quickly shift the SEALs from fighting a known enemy—taking out an evil dictator— to an unknown and complex insurgency.

This is when I came into the picture.

In early 2004 I was at the University of San Diego pursuing that PhD in leadership and teaching as an adjunct professor. The professorship was part time, so I was also building my next business, NavySEALS.com, on the side. I was not planning on going to war, either—that is, until I got a call from O'Connell. He asked me to come back to active duty to help the country. I would not be able to turn this guy down.

I could have jumped into the fray several years earlier, but held off because my business, job, family, and education needed me home. But I knew I was going to get recalled at some point, and there is never a perfect day to go to war. I had to break my own glass, which I gladly did for the captain and the mission.

O'Connell's team felt I was the right guy to lead a research project calling for a SEAL officer who both knew how to fight (or at least not get killed) and understood qualitative research methods.

The project was part research, part warfighting, and I was intrigued. Shortly after 9/11, the Marines saw that this new war was going to be led by the Special Operations Command (SOCOM). They were nervous about being sidelined. Vast funding and new technologies were rushing into the special ops teams, and the Marines were being left out in the cold. They wanted in, but Secretary of Defense Donald Rumsfeld wasn't going to hand it to them on a platter. It would be a fight—something Marines are very good at. The concept needed to be studied carefully, to see if their operators had the unique mindset to work in the murky special operations world.

The Marines are part of the Navy, and as such, Rumsfeld directed the Navy to perform a study to validate this concept. The Navy turned to the SEALs and said, "You own this." The Marines put together a hundred-man unit known as the Marine Special Operations Command Detachment One, or SOCOM Det 1 for short, and assigned them to SEAL Team One, which reported to O'Connell. He brought me in to study them.

My first task was to lead a complicated certification exercise to prepare the combined team for war. I would run the exercise while simultaneously studying the effectiveness of the Marines. The event was a dynamic ten days during which the SEALs, with attached Marines, would demonstrate that they were capable of working together in simulated counterinsurgency combat. My study was to start there, then continue as I followed them to Iraq and the Joint Special Operations Task Force in Baghdad. We were deploying thirty days after the training.

You might be asking yourself what any of this has to do with respect.

I'm getting there. It was clear from the outset that this whole project was a political hot potato. There was no love in the SEAL hierarchy for the idea of Marines coming into their turf. There was legitimate concern that the Marines would take money and missions away from the SEALs, as both units were to be maritime special forces within the SOCOM family.

A number of senior SEALs and some of the Navy brass looked to O'Connell to squash the initiative by making it impossible for the Marines to succeed. I was able to observe how O'Connell dealt with the tricky situation. What I saw was how respect plays a crucial role in authentic leadership.

Mr. O'Connell was an authentic leader with a broad perspective. He was humble, courageous, and trustworthy, and also incredibly clear on what his duty was. He didn't play politics, and I observed no personal agenda aside from his being 100 percent aligned with what was best for the country. The SOCOM Det 1 proof of concept received the fairest chance it could possibly have had. He knew it was up to the Marines to prove themselves and wasn't going to allow his team to obstruct their opportunity.

Just a few months before I deployed with the combined team, President George W. Bush declared victory, and most in the West considered the war over. The SEALs and Marines were going to go in to clean up loose ends and train some Iraqi SOF troops. Then we would all get to go home to our families.

Not a chance.

Things started to go sideways fast after we got to Baghdad. The troops faced a growing threat of improvised explosive devices (IEDs), suicide-vested civilians, mortar attacks on the forward operating bases, and roadside ambushes. The military found themselves in a new war, one that grew out of the original one. It was the most VUCA situation they had seen since Mogadishu or Vietnam.

It was going to require a complete reassessment of how to fight and win.

Meantime, the Marine detachment was cocksure and ready to get in the fight. Mobility by ground was a big deal for the maritime special ops in this environment. In the past, the SEALs would get where they needed to go on foot or by parachute, boat, or submarine. This time was different, so they got the best ground mobility they could conceive of. Taking inspiration from the British Long Range Desert Group of World War II fame, the Marines acquired vehicles suitable for the Iraq desert—called the Mercedes IFAVs.

Unfortunately, they chose poorly.

The fighting was now concentrated in the urban areas, yet the thin-skinned IFAVs were built for remote desert operations, as in the real desert. Their light bodies made them perfect for long-haul travel across the drifting sands. However, there was not much sand in Baghdad. The trucks and the crew could be destroyed in their first ambush. The fact that the vehicles were useless on day one put the entire Marine mission in jeopardy. It would take months to get new vehicles procured and sent over from the States. The proof of concept would be over by then, and the Marines shit out of luck.

At least they would have been had it not been for Captain O'Connell.

He recognized that these guys had made a "new guy" mistake. They deserved a fair shake and he was going to give it to them. He directed SEAL Team One to shake the local Humvee trees to get the Marines some vehicles. Within days, twelve Humvees drove into the joint SEAL-Marine compound. The teams quickly armored up the new rigs, readying them for their new mission.

Due in no small part to O'Connell's respect for the real team, the good ol' U.S. of A., the Marines succeeded in their proof of concept. His actions brought great respect to him from the men doing the fighting. He pulled their asses out of a sling, with nothing asked in return. It was the right thing to do.

Respect like that is built upon three key character traits: *integrity, authenticity,* and *clarity.*

Let's look at those three traits in more detail.

INTEGRITY

O'Connell knew what the team's mission was and that his personal views should not interfere. He was a warfighter and a man of high integrity. He wanted the Marines to have an equal chance, so he bent over backward to ensure they had the tools to succeed. The rest was up to them. Integrity leads to clarity of intention and communication.

Integrity is the most crucial element of respect, requiring great discipline and a strong moral compass. The lack of either can quickly erode respect. One definition of integrity is to be internally consistent, undivided. Some have argued that Adolf Hitler possessed integrity, because he was internally consistent in terms of what he thought, said, and did. To me, this definition of integrity is incomplete, because the notion of a positive moral drive is not built into it.

In my view, integrity is to be honest and internally consistent, while backing those strengths with moral uprightness. It takes discipline to think, speak, and act with a goodness of character. That moral compass compels you to do the good *and* the right things, while also ensuring the least harm to yourself, as well as to those not aligned with your actions.

To display this level of disciplined integrity requires that you be integrated yourself. What I mean by this is that you are willing to take a stand for what is right rather than what is expedient or good for your career or what you are pressured or ordered to do. If you are involved in something you sense is morally wrong, you won't hesitate to communicate it. And that communication is followed by action. Then you stand by your words and actions.

That is what I observed in O'Connell, and also why he was so well respected.

The communication methods of a leader with this level of integrity are different from those of others. Such a leader's words and the manner of their delivery are as accurate and clear as possible. He or she takes ownership of personal assertions or declarations about the past, present, and the future, such as "This is my perspective on what happened," or "This is the way I see things now," or "This is how I want things to be." An assertion is a statement of one's personal view of the facts. A declaration is a statement of one's stand or desired end state. Both require an abundance of self-awareness and a careful choice of words.

Mr. O'Connell was that clear and accurate with his communications. He made sure that what he was asserting or declaring was as true as possible. Not only was what he said perceived as accurate, but it was also received as useful, specific, and actionable.

There was simply no bullshit.

This principle of communicating integrity brings great respect to an individual from his or her team. Why? Well, obviously, because the members of the team are the ones most impacted by the words. They can appreciate the thoughtfulness because their lives and careers are on the line. Staring down the wolf means to rid yourself of emotional baggage so you can communicate in a true and accurate manner—with declarations, assertions, requests, offers, and promises that are useful, specific, and actionable. This requires a great deal of discernment. But there is another important element.

What you say must also be positive.

Communicating with negative energy is a real downer for the team. You can't be the negative apple in the bunch. Negativity destroys motivation and performance. It also weakens you as an individual. Your words must not be passive-aggressive or delivered with disrespect. The communication must be utterly positive and come from your open heart, even if you are not happy. Showing up day in and day out with a sense of how your energy and words impact the team is a powerful exercise in self-awareness. It will deepen your connection with your team and improve their over-all reliability. It will also quickly expose any negative conditioning from other teammates that is diminishing respect. The team will gain great clarity, and better understanding, because they will ac-tually listen to everything you say, instead of mentally checking out or expecting another negative dump. Indeed, the SEAL ethos of "earn your trident every day" includes how you communicate with your team.

The trident is the Navy SEAL insignia, and it has to be earned every day. One of the ways we did it—and you will as well—is by thinking, speaking, and acting positively and with disciplined integrity.

AUTHENTICITY

We have seen how integrity is about developing the discipline to speak and act with a moral compass, and how it requires self-awareness and control. So what does it mean to be authentic, then? Authenticity is present when leaders are real as they com-municate with their teams—not bullshitting anyone, including themselves. Whereas integrity relates to communicating and per-forming an act, authenticity is about being emotionally available, and in an "I-we" as opposed to a "me-them" relationship.

Authenticity relieves the leader from the burden of wearing masks because they fear judgment.

When leaders are inconsistent with how they communicate or

deal with different types of situations and people, it is a real problem. Wearing one mask with one group of people and a different one with another group simply doesn't work well. To be authentic is to be consistent no matter whose presence you are in or what the situation is. If I pretend to be authentic with my team but am acting as a careerist with those above me in the chain of command, then my team will see through that mask immediately. They will question my intentions and integrity. When I act all personally connected with them, they will think it's just another mask. This cancels out the positive power of one's work.

Respect is denied when you fear judgment.

The building of teams on a foundation of respect is hard work, but it is worth it.

In the military, I saw many leaders who espoused integrity, but acted one way with their peers and a different way with their subordinates; or they showed one set of facts to their officers and different one to their enlisted men; or they behaved one way with their teammates and a wholly different way when they were home with their family. True authenticity, the kind that brings deep respect, has no need for role masks.

I have worked hard at being in integrity with my teammates, bosses, wife and son, and so on. It requires that I pay attention to fear wolf patterns that had prompted me to put a mask on in the first place. It tripped me up in the Navy when I believed that to be authentic with my enlisted teammates, I had to party with them. That wasn't true, and it got me fired. False identities—with roots as deep as childhood—cause us to show up masking our authenticity.

Taking off the masks for good is liberating.

Doing so requires a healthy regard for yourself, something that many do not feel. In my work with executives and professionals from all walks of life, I have often seen subconscious shame, guilt, and feelings of unworthiness hold them back. They are successful professionally and financially, but are not content. The feelings of low esteem result from hurtful treatment by parents, peers, or other powerful people early in their lives. This led to emotional trauma and the experience of unworthiness—of not being lovable at a deep subconscious level.

Such things are generally not spoken of in offices and boardrooms. But in my leadership development work, I have seen many leaders and teams open their hearts to one another, and most share some story like this. That is how the healing begins. Watching their transformation is quite extraordinary.

Nobody is immune to trauma. A good friend of mine, Josh Mantz, served on the board of our Courage Foundation, which supports veterans with post-traumatic stress. Josh was killed in combat. Yes, he actually died, and then was resurrected quite surprisingly after a lot of loving work by his medical team—and fifteen minutes of flatlining. He is fond of saying that trauma does not discriminate, and that his most difficult trauma was from childhood—not from dying in combat. Powerful testimony.

The Hoffman Process is a world-renowned program for emotional development. The founder, the late Bob Hoffman, believed that most emotional shadow results from childhood trauma, which he called the *negative love syndrome.* Hoffman proposed that the absence or withholding of love due to emotional abuse, emotional blackmail, absence, addiction and other parenting limitations leads to trauma in undifferentiated and completely vulnerable children. It is common for the child to then suppress, adopt, or rebel against the "negative love" behavior. As children mature they develop negative reactionary patterns to the trauma as shadow aspects of their personality. Nobody, not even a SEAL the most skilled CEO—or even the president of the United States—can claim immunity from negative love syndrome. The good news is that it is possible to overcome those shadows with awareness and effort.

But most do not.

The sooner you can appreciate your own limitations and become aware of your shadow, the sooner you can start to integrate and become more authentic, and free.

One outcome of emotional work at this level is deep respect for your own imperfections, and yet goodness, as a human being. You cannot truly respect others if you don't first respect yourself. Awareness and healing are achieved through meditation and a competent therapist or an emotional development program such as the Hoffman Process (www.hoffmaninstitute.org) or the Q Process (see www.theQEffect.com). Shadow work as a personal practice is possible using EMDR therapy, which is having success in healing veterans suffering from the trauma of combat. (EMDR is short for Eye Movement Desensitization and Reprocessing. See *Getting Past Your Past* by Francine Shapiro, PhD, the creator of EMDR.) I highly recommend a combination of a deep intensive workshop, followed by therapy and self-care. You can build the self-care into your daily practice of contemplation and meditation. These practices help with reintegration of the parts of our personality that were split off in our earliest years, when we lacked the skills or awareness that we possess now.

Authenticity causes us to behave in a manner worthy of respect. An inauthentic person will expect others to live up to a standard, but will cut themselves slack with a myriad of excuses. Too exhausted, too overworked, already done that, deserve better, don't deserve better—you name your excuses here. Pay attention to what triggers you in your team or bosses. As the experts say, "if you spot it in others, you got it in yourself." Being respectable requires doing the work of emotional awareness and reintegration, while not judging or comparing your efforts, or results, to others. And you must stop beating yourself up when you slip up; the work requires patience and repetition.

Authenticity demands that you maintain internal balance, too. It is hard to focus on emotional development when you are out of balance, in poor shape, and stressed out. Staring down the wolf requires that you get physically fit, dial in your nutritional needs, enjoy seven to eight hours of quality sleep a night, and master the breathing skills for stress management. Maintaining control of your internal environment in this way allows you to respond positively, rather than react negatively, to the endless stresses of life. It helps you keep the masks off and locked in the closet.

Authenticity is also expressed as genuineness of character.

Do you truly, deeply care for your teammates? Captain O'Connell had a way about him that just *felt* fair and genuinely caring. I could sense that he was speaking from the heart, and not stuck in his head, dodging or obscuring the truth in any way. He had no hidden agenda even when doling out painful medicine. McRaven had this quality as well—I genuinely felt he cared about me even when he handed me my ass on a platter.

O'Connell left his door open and would put down whatever he was working on to deal with the incoming visitor, right then and there. The rank or role of the individual didn't matter; O'Connell treated everyone equally and with respect. He was as comfortable with the lower-ranked enlisted SEAL as he was with the admiral. That genuineness is a powerful quality of authenticity.

Authenticity also means being open to the ideas of others, accepting that they might be right and you might be wrong. Leaders who are open-minded drop the urge to be right all the time. Righteousness—needing to have the last word or ignoring the ideas of others—kills respect. Openness means more ideas are available and truly considered, leading to more perspectives and better decisions for the team.

Finally, authenticity isn't a rigid way of being. Flexibility—the willingness to evolve as you change, your team changes, and the world changes—is important. Authentic leaders expect that change is ongoing and are not fixed in their choices or rooted in past behaviors.

Be eager for change.

CLARITY

Clarity is critical for communicating with integrity. Clarity arises from a rigorous analysis of your intentions, both explicit and implicit. If a leader lacks clarity on the important aspects of a mission, it's possible *something* might get accomplished, but not necessarily what was expected. A leader must get clear on what his or her full intentions are—including what outcomes are desirable or even acceptable. In analyzing intentions, be aware that many are hidden in the domain of the fear wolf. These include those pesky biases that plague our thinking. Once you root these out, you move them from implied yet unstated and desired outcomes to explicitly stated outcomes. Or equally likely, you uncover undesirable expectations and avoid the negative consequences.

In the case of O'Connell, he was clear that one of his missions was to be the host for the SOCOM Det 1 proof of concept. That was explicitly defined. However, there were implied intents from his bosses that were not spoken of or agreed upon. So he was careful to pull as many of these to the surface as he could uncover. That way he and his team were clear about the actual mission and did whatever they could so the Marines had the tools they needed.

Captain O'Connell understood the hidden agenda and maintained respect while navigating it.

It is also important to be sure about what ultimate victory looks like. The team will need to understand what the bounty is and where the boundaries are in relation to the actual outcomes desired. Those things will guide behavior. When O'Connell told his team to "do whatever it takes" within legal confines to get appropriate vehicles for the Marines, he set an acceptable limit. He called his test to define boundaries the "*New York Times* test." He'd ask, "Am I willing to read about this in the next edition of *The New York Times*?"

I now employ that same test. Thank you, sir.

You must also be clear about what failure looks like. Even if your team is clear about the intent, the objectives, and the acceptable limits, they may not know what it looks like when the mission has failed. Leaders who provide that clarity to their team tend to garner greater respect, as it takes a deep level of introspection and humility to consider failure in advance.

Finally, respect requires that you be clear about the power and limits of your own role as a leader—the influence that you wield over others, the outsize energy your presence consumes, and the perspectives you need to take in order to be effective. I've witnessed a number of leaders lose the respect of their team because they didn't handle the power of their position well. One overplayed his hand, and another was weak, allowing or causing others to assume the lead. These leaders didn't demonstrate awareness of, or skillful use of, their power. They couldn't see things from anyone's point of view but their own.

RACE TO THE DEATH

I first met Joe De Sena in late 2014. He invited me to observe a new endurance race project, an area I was an expert in.

Joe loved long and painful events, having a passion for the

self-confidence and growth that training-induced suffering brings about. He decided to invite other like-minded nuts to his farm for a "Death Race." It was to last four days—well, actually until completion. He warned participants: "I don't recommend you do this race. You might die."

Nobody did, and they wanted more.

The Death Race evolved into the hugely successful Spartan obstacle racing company that he leads today. Joe invented a new sport from his passion, replete with its own televised world championship. In an attempt to expand and scale his business, he thought he would certify some Spartan coaches. He hired a few individuals to coordinate an event to take place at his farm in Vermont. Along with those individuals, he invited me and some other experts who had created unique training systems that closely aligned with his philosophy. Joe wanted our help in validating his training concept; he wished us to be his certifying "board of advisors."

I could see that Joe was clear about his mission. Launching the certification to help his business was the explicit objective. But he also made clear many implicit agendas backing that mission. The biggest was that quality was more important than quantity. It wasn't necessary to certify any of the hardy warriors who accepted his invitation. There were twelve candidates, all of whom expected to get certified that weekend. He made it clear that it was entirely possible they could leave empty-handed.

Joe articulated the standards of excellence. He was clear about the level of challenge the participants should expect. They would train for forty-eight hours without sleep. They would be moving constantly, doing difficult tasks and demonstrating their ability to both do and teach, and they would not know their schedule from one hour to the next. The focus was not so much on their knowledge as it was on their strength of character. This was right up my alley, and similar to our SEALFIT fifty-hour training event called Kokoro.

I witnessed Joe's integrity, clarity, and authenticity during the event. He had a team running the activities, and it would have been easy for him to go home when he was exhausted to put his feet up and hang out with his family. He didn't. He stayed up with us and participated in every twist and turn with the students. In my experience, that's not something most leaders would do.

We enjoyed hiking endless trails, tossing massive rocks, scaling a steep mountain, chopping cords of fire wood, and even doing two hours of hot yoga. Through it all we were observing the students closely.

He never put himself on a pedestal or set himself apart as the exalted founder of the Spartan Race. He was genuine and he displayed great respect for all participants and staff. Being willing to do exactly what he was asking his team and students do created an obvious affection between each. He was well loved by his team.

Exhausted and euphoric, we sat on logs at the end of the event, wondering if we would need to split those, too. Then, after we had carefully interviewed each of the students, Joe excused them and asked us what we thought.

I wouldn't certify any of them . . . yet, I told him. I didn't think they were ready to be his vanguard coaches. And though the experience was a gut check, as a certifying event it lacked the cohesive structure for a training model that would allow the coaches to teach others the lifestyle that Joe was promoting. Some of the experts agreed, while others were silent.

Joe didn't certify a single one of them.

It would have been easy for him to give them a consolation prize for enduring the test, but that would have been a breach of his integrity. He would not have been acting authentically. He had established quite clearly that they might not get certified, and he followed through when the results were in. He did not cave to the codependent pull to not hurt their feelings. He also took our input on the program and came at it later with a new approach. The certified coach program is thriving to this day, and Joe continues to be highly respected within his organization.

STILL FUBAR

Looking back at how my journey had progressed, you'd think that by now I'd have a success story in building my own elite teams in the corporate world.

Not so much. I appeared to be, as we used to say in the SEALs, FUBAR, or "fucked up beyond all repair."

Before I was mobilized to active duty by Captain O'Connell, I was developing the side business NavySEALS.com. I lacked the confidence to do the tech and marketing for it myself, so I partnered with a company to build the website and manage online sales fulfillment. I was basically outsourcing the e-commerce aspect of the business to them, which was practically the whole business at the time. I didn't do much due diligence on the company since I was working another job with the wife of the founder, and trusted her. The company was experienced in online operations and selling, which at that time was a new field. The reality was that I was feeding my fear wolf because I felt incompetent with the new internet technology. This pattern of self-doubt was a shadow of mine. It was true that I knew *nothing* about e-commerce and needed help in building the platform. But I didn't even try to research it or give other options a try. Instead I just trusted their expertise and signed a deal, without legal advice, to outsource most operational functions to them.

The partners started investing time and money in making the business successful, yet a few months into the relationship I began to sense that this partnership was not going to go well. Our values did not appear to be in alignment, an assessment I made based on the difficulty I had communicating with them and understanding their reporting. Distracted by the 9/11 attack and my growing commitments with the SEAL reserves, I ignored some important details. But my gut kept telling me I had a problem. Finally, I developed the courage to have a blunt conversation with them about the explicit and implicit assumptions in our agreement.

The devil is not just in the details; sometimes it's in the white space between the details. I had given up too much control and felt like they were taking over my business one piece at a time. I brought in a financial expert to help me work things out with them, but that went over like the boat in Morro Bay.

The intervention turned into a pissing match, and few days later I got a call from the domain hosting firm, informing me that the partner had contacted them, asking to transfer the NavySEALS .com domain, which I owned, to them.

My new partners apparently felt that they had rights to the domain as part of our relationship. That was not my understanding, and I had no intention of relinquishing my ownership of the valuable asset.

My perspective was that they knew I wanted out of the deal, so they were trying to take control of the domain to protect their investment. I immediately terminated the contract, and of course they hired attorneys. For a final kick in the gut, I had to pay them to get out of the deal.

A month later, they had re-created the business under a new domain name. Their new business was identical to mine. They simply had to change out the domain name and modify the website a bit. They took the concept *and* then stomped me by out-executing my small operation while I went off to war.

It was again my fault. I lacked clarity about my intentions and didn't validate for integrity.

I wasn't clear about why I needed the partnership to begin with. I wasn't clear in communicating the boundaries around ownership of the domain name. I even lacked clarity about the vision for the business. I *was* trying to be authentic, but that wasn't enough, and the entire thing blew up in my face. I created a legal mess and a competitor because I lacked clarity.

Respect was lost across the board.

I failed with the commitment to courage in the brewery. I fell down on the commitment to trust with the adventure company. And I blew the commitment to respect in this latest endeavor. Was I ever going to succeed in building an elite team in the business world? I guess I still needed to grow up and clean up more.

In spite of the failures, all of those experiences taught me how important a rigorous focus on one's own growth is—and how working with teams is one of the most potent opportunities for growth.

Let's discover how to leverage your team to accelerate growth.

SDTW Exercise 4:
INTEGRITY, AUTHENTICITY, AND CLARITY

Grab your journal and prepare your mind as in the previous exercises. When ready, perform the following:

STEP 1. Visualize a past experience in which you behaved in a way that lost you respect. What decisions did you make, and how did you react in a conditioned way that caused harm to yourself or others? Play the mental video for a few moments of that scenario, then journal your insights by answering these questions and recording any other insights that come up.

What does it feel like?
What did you learn?
Has the scenario happened more than once—i.e., is it a pattern?
What mask were you wearing? For instance, were you wearing a mask because you feared judgment or because you feared incompetence?
How did you fail on integrity, authenticity, or clarity?

STEP 2. Visualize yourself in your ideal physical, mental, and emotional state. See yourself acting in a creative, responsive way with disciplined moral integrity, deep authenticity (no masks), and absolute clarity in your communications. See how your team and family respond to you with great respect. See yourself as a respectable leader expressing yourself powerfully in thoughts, words, and deeds.

What does that feel like?
What did you learn? Where are the gaps between the old self and this ideal self?
How can you improve your integrity, authenticity, and clarity?

LEADERSHIP
COMMITMENT
#4

COMMIT TO
GROWTH

STARE DOWN THE FEAR OF DISCOMFORT

It's June of 1990, and I'm in hell.

SEAL training is nine months long—six months of BUD/S (Basic Underwater Demolition/SEAL Training) and three months of SEAL Qualification Training, or SQT. Throughout that time there are also leadership, survival, evasion, resistance and escape (SERE), and parachuting schools to fit in. Those who endure all this with courage and gain the trust and respect of their peers, earn the right to wear the trident. Then they report to their unit to start their training all over again with a new team. Being a SEAL is a long and never-ending process of training and growing, interrupted by periods of intense and brutal missions.

There are several training models deployed in BUD/S. Their purpose is to develop the skills and character of the new recruits to be an elite special operator. The basic skills are those things such as running, jumping, climbing, swimming, fighting, and such, along with tactical team skills such as shooting, moving, communicating, diving, explosives, small boat handling, and more. These are what I call *horizontal skills,* in that they improve you in a way that gives you the capacity to do your job better but won't necessarily change your character, who you are as a person.

Character training is not measured in accruing those horizontal skills. Rather, it is curated by challenging the thinking quality, moral compass, compassion, and perspectives of the student. The masterful SEAL instructors create scenarios and incidents that test decision-making under extreme pressure and in moral obscurity. The most famous example of this model, which plays out over one very long and painful six-day period, is called Hell Week.

A crucible is a container in which metals are subjected to extremely high temperature to transform them into another form. It is also a term for a severe trial in which different elements interact, leading to the creation of something new, such as relationships forged in the crucible of war. This definition fits Hell Week. It is a container in which to heat students to their transformation point, a severe trial introducing new elements that can forge the character of the students into something new.

The six days and five nights of around-the-clock hell burns off weakness and fear, and forges a team bond that is hard to create in any other way.

Of the hundred and eighty-five hard-core trainees who started in my BUD/S class, only seventy or so made it to the start of Hell Week. During Hell Week we lost another forty, and as I mentioned earlier, only nineteen graduated. Of the hundred and sixty-six who failed, some lacked resiliency, others got injured, but most failed because of something worse—they could not bear the temporary pain of the extreme discomfort that their transformation required. Those who failed would likely agree with me that *the temporary pain of transformation is far better than the long-term pain of regret.*

Hell Week is undoubtably one of the more unique transformational training programs. Aspects of it have been emulated by other elite special operations units, and many civilians have sought to experience its power through mini Hell Weeks such as SEALFIT's fifty-hour Kokoro crucible.

After two days without sleep, trainees who have left a subconscious back door open begin to question their reasons for being there. Those who came to BUD/S to prove that they're one of the toughest badasses in the world suddenly find that this doesn't really mean much to them anymore. Many simply can't recall why they were driven to be there in the first place. So these individuals quit and deny themselves the transformative impact of the crucible.

In order to make it through, students must be able to withstand discomfort and to look inside to confirm that "I'm meant for this; I am worthy of this." They must have a "no quit" attitude that carries them to hell and back again. That level of commitment and the courage to endure the experience can develop their character as a result. Students begin Hell Week at one level and exit as a different person—stronger, more aware, and a better teammate.

Enter my story of the Horra.

There were many guys in my class who early on I thought were capable of handling the stress and chaos, but lacked some other hard-to-define quality. One of these candidates was nicknamed "the Horra," a reference to the cult movie *Apocalypse Now*. In that film, Marlon Brando plays an Army Special Forces officer who apparently had lost his mind. In one scene he is heard chanting, "The horror, the horror." At any rate, the Horra had a name that sounded similar, and as you will see from this story, he also appeared to lose his mind, at least temporarily.

The Horra was physically fit and had the basic stuff necessary to be a SEAL—but from my perspective he seemed to be walking through the training in a bit of a daze. It was as though he was just getting by in each evolution, and slipping through the cracks unnoticed by the instructor cadre. I didn't think he would make it through Hell Week.

Hell Week starts on a Sunday and ends some time the following Friday. They don't tell you exactly when it will begin or end, but you sure can't miss it. A sudden barrage of weapons fire, smoke grenades, exploding bombs, sirens, and fire hoses foreshadows absolute chaos for hours. There are nonstop challenges, and the instructors seek to wear you down fast.

Drop down. Stand up. Drop down. Roll over. Crawl to the beach. Hit the surf. Crawl back. Push-ups. Endless, endless push-ups with water in your face the entire time.

And then the real training begins.

After the first two days and nights with no sleep, my class settled into a new normal—constant performance pressure, intense exhaustion, and plodding to the next meal. I was relying 100 percent on the mental skills I had learned in my Zen work—using breath control and positive self-talk, visualizing success, and maintaining presence. And I collapsed time to focus on micro-goals, as the instructors had advised. Those skills were money, and many students didn't have them.

Around eleven A.M. on Thursday of that week, the class came in from the predawn fun utterly spent. That night had been a long hallucinatory paddle around the island of Coronado, with endless drills in the sand dunes off Imperial Beach. The cold Pacific ocean water, open sores, and sand in places we didn't know existed were constant companions. The instructors advised that we'd done a great job and were to be rewarded with a hot shower and four hours of sleep. That seemed like a lifetime—but first we had to write a letter home to Mom. Everyone hunkered down over desks in warm and dry uniforms—in the overly heated classroom—and put pen to paper. Within moments, the only sound heard was Zzzzzz.

Then all hell broke loose again.

Of course they had been screwing with us. Forty minutes was

just enough time to slip into deep REM sleep after being awake for five days. This wasn't an exercise in hazing. Hell Week, while testing your mental and physical fortitude, is designed to simulate the conditions that a SEAL would experience in combat. There you won't know when your next meal is coming, nor when you would get your next opportunity to sleep, as you are exposed to constant chaos. You're not in control of anything except your ability to respond to the events as they come at you, and sleep deprivation can take even that away.

I slipped into deep sleep, thinking I was safe for four hours, when VUCA found us again—the sounds of machine guns, smoke grenades, and screaming instructors. I had to shake off the cobwebs quickly as the class hit the surf, transitioning from a dead sleep to the frigid ocean water in one minute. I rallied my boat crew, and as I moved out, I saw the Horra, looking even more dazed and confused. Someone had hauled him out of his seat and onto his feet, but he was just barely there. He looked as though he was in some faraway zone and began to walk into walls, bouncing off of them like a zombie, until someone pulled him outside. Once there, he wandered around while the rest of us raced toward the surf zone. When he didn't snap out of it, the instructors started in on him, shouting for him to move his ass. He didn't even acknowledge them. No lights were on, apparently.

The medics loaded him up in their medical van and took him to the clinic. There he would be assessed and rolled out of training as a medical drop. He'd proven that if this had been a combat situation, he'd have jeopardized the team and the mission, perhaps even been killed. Something inside the Horra's semi-functioning brain must have registered that reality, because he suddenly snapped to, staring at the ceiling of a van. It dawned on him where he was and what it meant, and as the vehicle rolled to a stop, he opened the door, jumped out to a perfect roll across the pavement, and sprinted back across the base.

His route took him back into the BUD/S compound and straight into the water with his boat crew. The instructors looked at him and at one another in amazement, their eyes asking if they should stop the madman. The head instructor just smiled and shrugged his shoulders as they let him jump into the surf. SEAL instructors are always on the lookout for uncommon resolve, students who break the status quo without breaking themselves, or the law.

They had just witnessed it.

The Horra had experienced a literal awakening from his "nap" and a deeper awakening to his purpose. He had the realization that his sleep-deprived mind had almost blown his chance to be a SEAL. He was smart, but had not yet developed the discipline to control his internal environment. However, something sparked a transformation in that moment, similar to what happens when people face a serious crisis. They can awaken to a bigger reality, a hidden source of power, and experience instantaneous change.

In other words, they grow up really fast.

As the Horra did. He finished Hell Week with the class and stepped up his game in all other aspects for the rest of training. He became a real leader and was one of the nineteen to earn the trident from class 170.

We'll revisit his story later in this chapter, but now I want to talk about the key elements of growth as it applies to leaders and their teams. Those elements are *challenge, variety,* and *mentors.*

CHALLENGE

We don't have to do Hell Week, but to grow to our fullest capacity as leaders, we must really challenge ourselves. We can't just stumble through any challenge, though. The types of challenges we take on, and our approach to them, are also important. Embracing meaningful challenges joyfully—showing up and working hard to become the very best version of yourself through the suffering—is key. That means getting out of your comfort zone and embracing discomfort to break the status quo that locks you in weak patterns.

I learned to love challenge first through gut-wrenching endurance sports like rowing and triathlons. Then it was the daily practice of the martial arts. Voluntarily attending the most severe military school on the planet was next. Today, hard functional exercise, aikido, yoga—with periodic gut checks to test myself—are standard operating procedure.

Challenging comfort is a lifestyle.

This lifestyle is inspiring and has attracted others who want to challenge themselves to train with me. In turn, these teammates push and prod my growth every day. Many military operators suffer when they leave their teams because they have nobody challenging them any longer. Through the Courage Foundation, we are helping vets see that they can again be part of a team committed to growth and serving each other. They can challenge themselves together to be their best again.

The development that comes from challenging yourself in this way is hard to put in words. It impacts every aspect of you as a leader. Greater integration, connection, and development toward the higher stages of conscious awareness result.

Setting the stage for accelerated development through challenges is one of the attributes of elite teams.

Challenging the whole of an individual leads to what we will call *vertical development,* as opposed to the *horizontal development* referred to earlier. This is personal growth that causes one to become more compassionate, aware, and capable. It is the type of character development that leads to a wider perspective and more nuanced decision-making.

Vertical development also leads one to become more inclusive and sensitive to others.

This is not the same as gaining new skills or getting better at doing something. That horizontal growth is useful for more efficient and effective execution. Horizontal growth doesn't evolve you as a person. Think of vertical growth as a ladder, where you're climbing to higher and higher stages of awareness, perspective, and sense of self.

As discussed in the introduction, we all have the capacity to experience three broad stages of vertical development: egocentric, ethnocentric, and world-centric. Ultimately, the objective with vertical growth is to move permanently to the world-centric stage of care and concern—that Fifth Plateau. Many are stuck at the stages of egocentrism and ethnocentrism, which encompass the first, second, and third plateaus (though many at the third plateau can be world-centric because business is global). My belief is that world-centric leadership is inevitable through accelerated development, when we unlock our full potential, as I am proposing in this book. It is a natural evolutionary step.

But it will take the team to get us there.

We may like to think that we're already enlightened and operating at our full potential. But that's not realistic thinking. To break free of patterns locking in our "old story" and limiting our potential, we must challenge everything that we think we know about ourselves. You can do this with the help of your team. The team can establish the conditions to bring forth greater authenticity among its members. This is accomplished with vertical development training.

That is how the Horra evolved, and how you and your team will as well.

Let me differentiate between ascending to a new stage of development and experiencing a temporary state that feels like one. SEALs are accustomed to accessing flow and peak states. Such states occur during intense experiences requiring the body, mind, and emotions to be completely in sync, while one's attention is directed toward a complex task. At some point, time seems to slow down or speed up, and one's actions flow in an effortless manner.

An acute awareness of one's surroundings ensues, along with a feeling of being deeply connected to others, nature, and the universe itself. Temporary state changes such as this can enhance one's performance, while leaving an internal "trail marker" to point the way to a higher stage of one's personal evolution.

This has happened to me on many occasions, both during my time in the SEALs and since. It didn't happen to me because I was special. It happened because my training prepared me for it, and the situation demanded that I show up with my whole being focused on a singular challenging task. But those experiences of flow or peak states were temporary and brought on by horizontal skill mastery. This is not the same as a vertical development stage shift. That plateau shift required that I develop more awareness, heart connection, and complex decision-making based on a new internal reality map. And that vertical growth was not accompanied by a state of flow or experienced as bliss. In fact, it can be somewhat uncomfortable as you discard your old beliefs and patterns. But that temporary discomfort is necessary to develop morally, emotionally, and spiritually.

There is pain associated with shedding the old skin.

It is imperative to challenge yourself to experience vertical growth together with your team. The corporate realm, for the last century, has been devoid of vertical development and any "heart-mind" training. But nowadays it is important to have a world-centric perspective, and as much care and concern for your board of directors and investors as you do for those in the mailroom or sweeping the tarmac. Everyone is important, everyone is connected, and everyone is fulfilling an important role. Only by challenging growth vertically can you fully embody these attributes.

Develop your capacity to be better at doing good *and* to do better at doing things.

Most leaders seek to hire character and train skills. That means they want to hire for potential and train for performance—hire those already committed to growth and then provide challenging horizontal training so those hired can master the tools of their trade.

That is a solid plan, but you can improve it: Hire for character, then train for both character and skills.

COMPOUNDING AND PROJECTION

A gifted yoga teacher once told me: "If you're not training on the edge of the mat, you're taking up too much space."

This most certainly applies to developing leadership and teaming capacity. You will want to push yourself to the edge to improve at least 1 percent every day. Seek to improve every task you take on and quality of each interaction by that 1 percent. That isn't much, but over time the impact will be dramatic. Train your mind to focus intently and be more present and engaged. Master the vertical development skills of breath control, concentration, meditation, and visualization through learning, doing, and teaching—using your entire being. With every repetition you can increase the level of challenge just a bit. This approach allows you to release the power of compounding in your developmental work.

Compounding your growth works in much the same way compound interest does in finances. You will see a high rate of return on your investment in growth by challenging yourself a little bit more each day. At first the results will accrue slowly. Soon enough you find yourself with significantly more leadership ability and team capacity, and overall success.

Vertical leadership growth also helps you project power much like the domino effect where small dominoes can lead to toppling a much larger ones due to the momentum. Let me use weapons training to describe the projection of power. You're handed a weapon you don't know how to handle; in fact maybe it scares the shit out of you. However, you have a mentor who shows you how to use it, and over time, you're able to hit a target at 25 yards; then the next thing you know, all of your bullets are landing at the center of the target at 100 yards; then you're doing it while walking and running. You compound your skills while projecting greater and greater power. All it takes is for you to knock that first domino down; then that domino will knock the next one down without any effort on your part, and so forth and so on. Soon you've toppled the whole chain of dominoes and the largest obstacle, one bigger than you could ever imagine when you started. Imagine that combination of compounding and projection playing out with your personal growth goals!

DON'T FORGET THE BASICS

Fundamental to the concept of challenge for growth is to be sure to come back to the basics often, no matter how advanced your skills get. With both horizontal and vertical skills, you have to keep working on the basics of your foundation. If we use the example of shooting again, the horizontal skill basics are your grip, your stance, your breathing, and your trigger pull. While advancing in all of the other aspects, you must continue to practice these basics, or you might not progress the way you want.

With vertical skills, such as emotional awareness and mindfulness, many have a tendency to leave the basics behind as they get attracted to shiny new training or hacks. The fundamentals then fall apart. You must examine what basic skills you need, and then stick to a simple set of tools to develop those.

For example, consistently practicing the basics of the skills I used during Hell Week and teach at Unbeatable Mind will have a profound impact. Here they are:

Skill 1. **BOX BREATHING** will bring you back into balance, able to control stress and calm your mind.

Skill 2. **POSITIVITY** will train you to maintain a positive mental and emotional state, always feeding the courage wolf. This has a tremendously positive impact on your peace of mind, self-esteem, and ability to team well.

Skill 3. **VISUALIZATION** of your future will turn it into destiny instead of a wish, while visualizing your past can help you eradicate regrets.

Skill 4. **FRONT SIGHT FOCUS** on your most crucial targets,

with micro-goals connected to your vision and mission, will take your performance and achievement through the roof.

Be aware that your ego can trick you to think you have "made it" and you don't need the training any longer. The ego will be your biggest obstacle to overcome. It's good to remember, as Gertrude Stein put it, that there's no there there—you are always in the process of becoming. The question is: Are you becoming whole and integrated as a world-centric leader, or are you becoming something less than that because you think you don't need to train or challenge yourself any longer?

COMMITTING TO THE CHALLENGE

Is there a best practice to challenging yourself every day? Where do you start? Why not begin by taking a close look at what comfort zones and ruts you are in right now.

Then challenge yourself to get out of them!

Have your team and mentor or coach help you identify those ruts. Some places my clients have identified where they could immediately implement strategies to improve include:

1. Spending a senseless amount of time on social media

2. Saying yes to too many things

3. Poor eating, sleeping, and exercise habits

4. Not doing their box breathing to eliminate stress

5. Reactionary thinking or emotional patterns that bring conversations to a halt and damage relationships

6. Contracting to a lower plateau when faced with conflict

7. Not knowing what they want, or having difficulty expressing it

There is so much opportunity to stare down the wolf and grow by challenging your ruts, biases, and conditioned patterns. Use the crawl-walk-run principle and start with just one pattern.

Then challenge yourself to do the exact opposite to overcome it.

Here is a simple example. I slowly overcame my tendency to say yes to everything by practicing saying no or "Let me think about" to *all* requests. This gave me the freedom to make more rational and emotionally grounded decisions. As I paused to step back from the charge of a situation where someone was making a request, when I was triggered to say yes, I could see more clearly what was right for me, instead of trying to please them or acting from a hidden fear. I became even more focused and had more time for the right things from this simple practice. As a bonus I didn't have to fulfill commitments I never should have made.

Remember, rutted, biased patterns run deep and will keep tripping you up until you overcome them. Focus first on breaking the patterns that drain your time and energy the most. That way you will see major breakthroughs and will have even more motivation for your vertical development training.

Make a deal with your teammates to challenge you every day on the biggest pattern you want to overcome. Turn this into a practice and you will be stunned by how fast you evolve.

VARIETY

When you are doing the same tasks day in and day out, you experience little to no variety. You see the same people in the same environment every day. The only thing that changes when you are promoted is the level of difficulty of the task. Of course you also may be under more stress.

Lack of variety will keep you stuck.

The Horra grew through the dual challenge of the SEALs and an extraordinarily wide variety of skills and jobs. I saw this readily after I left the Navy, and have turned variety into a growth practice. You must have variety in both personal and professional endeavors. You will benefit greatly by constantly exposing yourself to new things, new places, new people, and new ideas. Elements that introduce variety into your life include, for example, hobbies, academic courses, travel, adventures, and side gigs. These help you expand your horizons and keep you developing new neuroplastic pathways in your brain. If that variety is also challenging you to stare down your fears, such as taking up skydiving, rock climbing, or acting, then it will also help you develop greater confidence.

I have my coaching clients take on a new challenge each quarter and hold each other accountable. Some recently did an eight-week improv class—which scared the heck out of them. When it was over, they raved about the experiences, each overcoming fear and growing in important ways. From the standpoint of vertical development, variety develops new skills you didn't realize you would benefit from, and the exposure to new ideas and cultures brings expanded awareness into both your personal and professional arenas.

You can change things up frequently—but with a caveat. When it comes to a variety of professional experiences, you don't want to just skip along the surface, always experiencing new things at the expense of going deep into what the team or organization needs. I have seen clients run from one new thing to another, only to find themselves behind the power curve at the office. It is better to go deep into something new every one to two years than to try something new every month.

You are always training, even if it is unintentional. The people you hang with are also training you.

If you are not proactively training a new pattern of thinking and being, then you are training to improve the old worn-out patterns. And hanging with the same stuck people trains you to keep thinking the same stuck way. Variety spurs growth because it forces you to change up those you work with and hence train with. As you seek out new opportunities for learning, you will have to deal with new groups of people at different stages of development and with varying world views. They become an extension of your tribe—you're going to practice your new vertical skills with them. This keeps you sharp as you refine your style and learn new perspectives to fit in. Let's face it—if I was still training with the same seven men I went to BUD/S with, doing the same things, I'd be bored shitless (no offense, guys) and would have stopped growing a long time ago.

Variety in skill development is also important. Often companies do the same training over and over, expecting different results. Let's return to the shooting example. We started with the basics of breathing, grip, and stance. Then we practiced by dry firing, then live firing at increasing distance from the target. Next we added moving targets, and then we would move while the target moved to realistically simulate a gunfight. Variety was always present for the skills of being a SEAL.

Variety also means changing up the conditions in which you train. An example would be learning to shoot in the morning when the sun is low; during the middle of the day when it's hot; when it's pouring down rain; and in different geographies and climates. It's also about changing the situation in which you apply your skills, so that the conditions are less than ideal. What does it look like to utilize your vertical skills when things are falling apart all around you? That is when they pay big dividends.

Another way to experience variety as a leader is *not* to lead. Actively seek out situations in which you can step back and be a follower. Most of us are focused on being the leader, but being a follower has equal value. Leaders and followers are the yang and the yin of a team. Yes, you are a leader of leaders, but that may mean a lot of leaders striving to be in charge. In elite teams, everyone is both a leader *and* a follower, and the roles shift frequently and seamlessly.

Endeavor to be led as often as you lead.

If there are no followers, there is no one to lead. Being a good follower means constantly setting your ego aside and letting go of the need to be right or in charge. You will stop judging the effectiveness of the leadership of others, because you don't want them to do that to you. Instead, every instance of leadership, regardless of who is in charge, becomes an opportunity to improve the entire team's effectiveness. Being a good teammate will improve your coaching and mentoring skills as well. This dual leader-follower approach to your roles helps you to see all perspectives—an attribute of fifth plateau leading.

Teams that embrace variety grow faster together. The team can facilitate growth by introducing more challenge and variety into their work, whether it be learning new skills, taking on additional roles or new roles, or bringing in physical training, meditation and breathing exercises, and outside experts.

MENTORS

When I was a certified public accountant in New York before I joined the SEALs, I had zero professional mentors. I felt lost and embarrassingly incompetent. Then I met Zen master Tadashi Nakamura at Seido Karate on 23rd Street. His mentorship was not about doing things better. Rather, he began to show me how to *be* better as a person. Through Zen training, he gave me a peek into my own rutted patterns. It was through these experiences, and challenging me with a variety of new training practices, that I was even capable of conceiving of being a SEAL officer.

That is the power of one good mentor.

A mentor is someone who has traveled your path before you. Mentors offer guidance for a specific personal or professional need and without expectation of anything in return.

But I have learned that you will need a team of mentors. When I joined the SEALs, I found a peer mentor at SEAL Team Three named Mark Crampton. He was our senior enlisted chief and became a close friend. Mark helped me learn how to become a good officer—how to care for the troops, to be authentic and accessible, and to always have their back. He was a great peer mentor.

While I was being mentored by Mark, I was also being mentored by Commander McRaven. He was my boss, but our interactions made him also a mentor for me. He considered the mentoring of junior officers to be an important aspect of his job. He was a great example of a boss mentor.

Jerry Peterson—who developed and led the 300-hour course where I became an instructor in hand-to-hand combat—taught me to fight effectively, and also mentored me to develop an offensive mindset and intuitive spontaneity. Jerry was a great example of a teacher mentor.

When I left the SEALs and started the Coronado Brewing Company, I found myself again without any mentors—which meant I was about to experience embarrassing incompetence again. Any time I have tried to "go it alone" without a mentor, thinking I had it all figured out, I have been schooled. I learned of professional mentor organizations like Young Presidents' Organization (YPO) and Entrepreneurs' Organization (EO). I gained a team of mentors through their forum experience, meeting monthly with eight individuals deeply committed to supporting each other. As the CBC devolved into chaos, this team held up the mirror for me and helped me see things more clearly, enabling me to make better decisions and navigate my way through that mess.

I was able to contrast those experiences, both before and after the SEALs, and realized just how important mentorship is to growth. Because of that, I've committed to maintaining a team of mentors ever since. I also have a couple of other experts with whom I have periodic contact for coaching, which I discuss below.

Mentoring is not a one-way relationship. The mentor should receive as much value from the relationship as you do. Consider mentoring others as well; you will find it most rewarding. I provide this same type of mentoring with no expectation in return. It just makes me feel good to help others the way I was helped.

COACHES

Every leader also needs a coach, and more than one is a good idea. A coach has specific skills to help you with your growth and goal attainment—typically in a paid capacity. Effective coaching requires dedicated training, and the world is full of mediocre coaches. After all, there are over five hundred coach certification programs. There are coaches for physical training, nutrition, emotional development (also known as a therapist or counselor), leadership development, and life itself.

Seek out a coach based on your specific developmental needs. The coach can provide a custom mirror for you. In that mirror, you can see how you appear now in that developmental area and also over time. They will help you to see qualities that you want, but don't yet fully embody—or ones that you'd like to eradicate entirely.

A thoughtful analysis of your qualities will expose vertical development needs—necessary training for physical, emotional, and spiritual growth—as well as any horizontal skills you may want for career enhancement or change. Either way, you will want to work with those you resonate with, making sure they are qualified and have the skills you need. Even with a hired coach, the relationship should not feel transactional. You need to get authentic with your coach and open your heart and desires to him or her. Confidentiality is crucial. You want people invested in your development in a caring manner.

Coaches are found through the organizations that certify them and associations for coaches. But how to find a good one? The best place is where you work, in the form of someone you respect. Ask who coaches him or her. They can also be found through professional organizations that provide developmental services, such as Scaling up, Strategic Coach, and Unbeatable Mind. I have asked my friends and associates for referrals to the best coaches they have used. Coaches might also come in the form of teachers with whom you've taken seminars or trained with, such as a martial arts or yoga teacher.

In addition to helping you identify and support your developmental needs, good coaches will hold you accountable and will be brutally honest with you. They will help you to raise your own standards beyond what you might set for yourself. They should have your best interests at heart and be able to see the best version of you, even when you can't. They do not live with your set of limiting beliefs and should be able to see your potential better than you can. This is why they will help you raise your standards. When you fall down or you feel like you just can't go another step, your coach will provide you with the support necessary to get you up and keep you moving on.

Your coaches should also demonstrate excellence through their own actions. If they do not, then move on. They should show you what it looks like to perform at an elite level in their realm of expertise, so that you can learn from their example. This gives you a perspective you might not have considered. They are both a training partner and a teacher.

Leaders also need to coach their teams. That is why coaching is a valuable skill for a leader to develop. The seven skills we teach our Unbeatable Mind coaches are below. You can see how valuable these skills would be for any leader.

1. **Attention control**

2. **Embodied engagement**

3. **Powerful questioning**

4. Creating awareness

5. Direct communication

6. Designing and taking action

7. Managing progress

EPIC ADVENTURES

In 2019 I was invited by a member of the Aspen EO, Sheldon Wolitski, to work with his forum. Sheldon is founder and CEO of a large staffing company, and I was excited to see how he employs the principles of growth.

Every year he organizes an "Epic Adventure" for his top performing teammates. He brings in different challenges from training models such as SEALFIT and the Wim Hof Method to test his team with experiences radically different from what they find in their work setting. That year he did the event outdoors in the Colorado winter—where they proved how Wim Hof's breathing exercises helped develop enough body heat to stay warm in the freezing cold! This training was not just for a gut check, though. They were learning new tools and breaking old patterns, both of which are important for vertical character development as we have discussed. They were also sharing a unique experience and taking risks together, which leads to great team alignment. You may be thinking that these events are somewhat tortuous, but a team with the right attitude has a blast participating in them.

While Sheldon challenges his own team to grow, he continues

his own growth with a team of mentors and coaches. He belongs to both EO and YPO and engages a high-level executive coach. He receives informal mentoring from peers and experts he has networked with. Sheldon is a living example of the three aspects of growth discussed in this chapter: challenge, variety, and mentors.

THE HORRA GROWS UP

On a trip to Florence in 2014, Sandy and I visited the Uffizi Gallery to see the works of Italian artists like Raphael, Michelangelo, and Leonardo da Vinci. As we walked through the museum, I heard a voice call out, "Cyborg!" (my nickname in the SEALs). I hadn't heard that in a while.

I turned around and was shocked to see the Horra standing there behind me. I wondered what the odds were of running into him like this.

Twenty-four years after I last saw him in BUD/S training, he was now a master chief (the most senior enlisted rank) in the SEALs. His eyes had an unusual clearness and sharpness to them. He was incredibly poised. In our short conversation, I could see that his mind, his awareness, his curiosity and intellect—everything was advanced, keen. We talked about art, the state of the SEALs, and many current events. When we finished, we said our goodbyes and parted ways.

And I have not seen him since. But I have thought of him often.

I recall standing for a few moments struck by the contrast

between the Horra I'd known in SEAL training, the zombie I saw almost get rolled out of Hell Week, and the man I'd just spoken to. He was extraordinarily fit, and his physical appearance belied his actual age. From the awakening he'd had in the back of that medical van, to traveling the world experiencing challenge, variety, and the mentorship of the elite Navy SEALs, he'd experienced accelerated vertical development of the type I am advocating. He had grown into an authentic, integrated, and world-centric leader; he projected total excellence. It was inspiring to see.

Excellence is the next commitment of elite leaders and teams. We'll discuss how *curiosity, innovation,* and *simplicity* help you to develop and display a new level of excellence each and every day.

SDTW Exercise 5:
CHALLENGE, VARIETY, AND MENTORS

Grab your journal and prepare your mind as in the previous exercises. When ready, answer the following questions and reflect on how to close the gaps:

How do you challenge yourself in uncomfortable ways?

Do you have variety in your personal and professional life? How can you add more?

Do you have a mentor or team of mentors you trust, people who help guide your career?

Is there a gap in knowledge you could use help in closing with a mentor?

Do you have a gap in your performance? Would a performance or leadership coach be of benefit?

What is the current state of your body? Would you benefit from a physical fitness coach? What about a nutrition coach?

Who supports your emotional development? Do you have an emotional coach or therapist to guide you as you stare down the fear wolf?

What about your spirituality and alignment in life? Would a spiritual or life coach be of benefit?

Distill all this down to an actionable plan and commit to find one new mentor or coach.

LEADERSHIP COMMITMENT

COMMITMENT

#5

COMMIT TO
EXCELLENCE

STARE DOWN THE FEAR OF BEING UNIQUE

Most people by now have heard of SEAL Team Six. There are books and TV shows about this fabled unit, but officially it was disbanded. Not really—the name was changed, but the unit continues on. It is special because it was and still is an utterly unique display of excellence within a larger organization that thrives on excellence. Personally, I think the

Navy should just admit that nobody is fooled and go back to calling the unit SEAL Team Six. The story of how this incredible team came to be, and the man behind it, frames the commitment we will explore in this chapter.

The SEAL Teams were created by an executive order signed by John F. Kennedy in 1962. That order created SEAL Team One, based out of Coronado, California, and SEAL Team Two, out of Little Creek, Virginia. The requirement arose out of the nature of the unconventional proxy wars being waged between the United States and USSR. The United States feared the domino effect of regimes close to our sphere of influence aligning with the Soviets. This fear came to a head with the Cuban Missile Crisis, which the SEALs were part of.

Both new SEAL Teams were formed out of the legendary Underwater Demolition Teams (UDTs). Those units operated valiantly in World War II, in the Korean conflict, on countless secret intelligence ops against the Soviets, and even in the Gemini and Apollo space missions. One day a small contingent of UDT operators showed up at their team and got the new orders, and the next day they were part of a newly minted SEAL Team. Presto chango. The two teams went looking for new training tactics, procedures, and weaponry suitable for their new mission. The guidance was to get very creative, because the nature of warfare was changing fast.

The frogs were leaving the water and needed to find their legs on terra firma. The rest, as they say, is history.

From their inception, the SEALs have been a secretive group. They are uncomfortable with the publicity showered on their success (and failures) in the recent past. It is hard to put that genie back in the bottle. I wrote a lot about the history of the SEALs when I started NavySEALs.com in 1997. Acquiring the domain name for $35, I built the website that soon became an unofficial recruiting source and historical archive. That mission is now being handled extremely well by the Navy SEAL Museum and Foundation.

The active duty community wasn't very excited about NavySEALs.com. They preferred to remain hidden from view, and this new internet thing was troubling. My perspective was that someone was going to do it and that it should be a SEAL. I was right, and now there are many SEAL websites run by people who have never been in the military and are sometimes not even from the United States (you read how I inadvertently helped to create one of them). The Navy investigated whether they could just take the domain from me, even though other top military domains, such as Army.com, were also owned by civilians at the time. I offered to sell it directly to them, but they declined, instead fighting my effort to trademark the site. Eventually I got tired of not making any money off of it and moved on to train special ops candidates via SEALFIT. The Navy left me alone.

In the NavySEALS.com forums I found myself engaging in ridiculous arguments with anonymous keyboard tough guys who thought they had an inside scoop. The three topics that most often came up:

1. Everything to do with SEAL Team Six

2. Whether Jesse Ventura was a phony, and whether the UDT were SEALs

3. Actual phonies claiming to be SEALs

Let me just say publicly that while phony SEALs should be fined or jailed (and there are thousands of them), Jesse Ventura is not a phony. He was UDT, and SEALs consider the UDT to be SEALs, so Jesse was a SEAL. And SEAL Team Six was, and is, the most badass special ops unit ever.

There, enough said. Now where was I?

Oh, yeah. When the SEALs were formed in 1962, there were less than 200 hard-core pioneers. One of them was a rough-and-tumble operator named Richard Marcinko at SEAL Team One. He became the face for the new force when his profile appeared in the *Navy Times,* the first public story about the secretive new unit. The picture showed him in the jungle, his face camouflaged and wearing a tiger-striped beret. The title of the article caught everyone's attention: "The Men with Green Faces."

Marcinko had a green camo face in the photo and looked terrifying. His nickname was Demo Dick for his considerable talent in blowing shit up. He was already respected by his teammates as one of the most effective operators in the Vietnam conflict. That was his domain, where he would master his craft and innovate new ways to destroy the enemy.

The newly minted SEALs' mission in Vietnam was to disrupt supply lines and take down the leadership of the Viet Cong. The teams operated in small squads of four, six, or eight—and only at night. They developed unconventional methods of covertly infiltrating enemy territory. They used speed of movement, ambush, total silence, camouflage, subterfuge, and deception. They ditched the issued gear and secured or modified equipment and weaponry to work in the wet jungle environment.

The Viet Cong knew about Demo Dick. They were terrified of this new phantom threat—so much so that a bounty was placed on his head. They called the SEALs "Devils with Green Faces" (maybe they had a subscription to the *Navy Times*). Viet Cong unfortunate enough to encounter this force of nature told tales of demons materializing out of thin air to destroy entire units, then disappearing back into the darkness. That's how effective the SEALs were at stealth, surprise, and silence. Marcinko had found his calling and built his first elite team—at SEAL Team One.

After Vietnam, Marcinko went to college and received a commission as an officer. Years passed and he had a distinguished career that led him to the coveted commanding officer job at SEAL Team Two. While running secret ops against the Soviets, Marcinko also watched with concern the rise of the terrorist threat.

His SEAL Team Two operators visited all sorts of military units and bases as they moved about the world. In his travels he noticed a growing laxness in the handling of the security of strategic assets. Others' ideas of excellence did not mesh with his own, and he concluded there was a risk from terrorism to the U.S. military, both overseas and at home.

The sneaky SEALs are able to penetrate the best-designed defenses. They figured that a determined enemy would be able to do it to us, too. Marcinko decided to counter that threat—specifically to deploy his offensive tactics to improve the defense of the U.S. Navy, and the military writ large.

A Team Two "red team" was organized to test the security at U.S. military establishments. After all, the best defense is a good offense, and once the security gaps were brought to their attention, the military would happily improve them.

This was a utopian view.

Marcinko's small team penetrated a variety of bases and assets, often without the cooperation or knowledge of the local commanders, though the Department of Defense (DoD) was fully aware of Marcinko's exercises. Successful enemy attacks on U.S. assets overseas and at home years later proved his initiative to be prescient, albeit ahead of its time.

Marcinko was committed to excellence, but the bureaucracy was committed to preserving the status quo. He was criticized for using unconventional tactics, even though he had explicitly stated that these were the means to an end. For example, his men would dress up as security forces from the base and easily engage socially with the ship's security forces, gaining access. Sometimes they would stage distractions and gain access disguised as police officers or firemen. They'd falsify IDs to be used if challenged after sneaking up from the waterline. He would send his men in to "kidnap" commanding officers right from under the noses of their own security forces.

Needless to say, Demo Dick pissed off a lot of powerful people.

It did not deter his team, however, because as they uncovered glaring holes in the security forces, they were proving what they were truly capable of as a team. It was a way to keep the team sharp during the cold war, when real-world operations were sparse. Why not "practice" on our own forces? they reckoned. This paradigm continues to this day—Blue and Green Team good guys routinely square off against Red Team bad guys in simulated combat.

Marcinko had a deep curiosity about the techniques and technologies his team could develop to do their jobs. He pushed them to always adapt and improvise to do things better. Never satisfied with the way things were at any given point, his team sought to answer the question of what their next op, their next war, would require. While other teams were still training Vietnam-era SEAL tactics, he had his staff look at how other SOF units operated, those in the United States as well as those of allies *and* enemies. They tested the crap out of their new toys and methods of insertion and extraction.

Marcinko was an inveterate innovator, a trait that is a hallmark of excellence.

The Red Team initiative was so successful—and high profile, even if controversial—that it didn't fit within SEAL Team Two any longer. It was begging for its own command structure, so Demo Dick lobbied to have his small Red Team of six operators, nicknamed Mob Six, to be spun out to form the nucleus of a new special mission unit. This was not unlike a start-up spinning out of a larger corporation. The precedent was set when the Navy spun the SEALs out of the UDT. Marcinko didn't want to create a new special ops force within the Navy, but a new specialized unit within the SEALs—to take what they had built to a whole new level.

He saw the future—and was determined to build it.

As he relates in his memoir *Rogue Warrior,* Marcinko was able to pull some strings for the reallocation of funds from an aircraft that the Navy was going to buy, using them instead for the formation of this new team. Thus Mob Six became SEAL Team Six and Marcinko its first commanding officer.

SEAL Team Six wanted to be the best, and to recruit only the best of the best.

The new team had an important mission: countering terrorism and the proliferation of weapons of mass destruction. Marcinko threw out the old playbook and developed a rigorous selection process for new entrants to the team. You couldn't just get assigned to the team, which rankled the status quo careerists with visions of serving there. He required operators to be hand-selected and pass another arduous six-month training program called Green Team. New recruits, who all had five or more years as a SEAL already, still had to have the right mindset for this new team. Not all SEALs succeed at Green Team.

Demo Dick realized that technology was making the world smaller. His operators needed new clandestine ways of creeping into the bad guys' land. They had to get even sneakier. They continued the tradition of the pioneering SEALs of Teams One and Two by inventing SOPs for a new type of warfare.

The team developed all sorts of innovations during this period, tactics now common across all special ops forces. One example is the "high altitude, high opening" parachuting tactics used to penetrate hard-to-get-to places, commonly known as "hop and pop." They would mock up a military airline with a signature to look like a commercial plane and jump out at cruising height—36,000 feet—to perform the hop and pop. This required the SEALs to deploy their parachutes at that height and to fly a navigated path—which could be anywhere up to seventy miles into enemy territory—to touch down. They did this because radar can detect the metal signature of an airplane, but not that of a parachutist.

The elite SEALs also learned to drive, fly, and navigate just about anything with an engine. They became pilots, manned underwater sleds, flew remote unmanned drones, and drove ships and even large construction equipment. They taught themselves to make use of any type of equipment such that if they accessed an enemy installation, they could use whatever materials were available, similar to the antics in the television show *MacGyver*. In fact, the MacGyver character was based on Marcinko—a man who could do anything with bubble gum, rigger's tape, and a Swiss Army knife.

THE REAL ENEMY STRIKES

As Marcinko's exploits once again became legendary within the Navy, his enemies on the inside sharpened their swords.

Innovators rub second plateau protectors of the status quo the wrong way. They challenge the protectors' view of the world, which causes them to double down to protect their turf. Conformists often confuse excellence with elitism, and establishment gatekeepers push back. They fear innovation.

Marcinko didn't fear being unique. He wanted to break the status quo.

Marcinko needed the latest technology quickly. He couldn't write up a proposal for tech that would be developed eight years later by a corrupt procurement system. By then it would be completely useless. For example, the SEALs asked for a dry submersible capable of longer operations than the current SDV. The contract to build what became known as the ASDS, or Advanced SEAL Delivery System, was awarded to Northrop Grumman, an aircraft builder. Makes perfect sense. After one mission, the batteries exploded, and the billion-dollar fiasco ended. Marcinko wanted to avoid idiocy like that, and he did so at a high cost.

He had his team procure off-the-shelf technology. But the Navy, with its stringent procurement guidelines, was not set up with the financial process to do this. It was mission critical, so Demo Dick felt he was in his rights to use the command credit cards, a "creative financing" method. It was all for the fight, he reasoned—the bean counters could figure out which bucket to put the beans into. The tactic crossed the bureaucracy's legal lines and gave his enemies the ammo necessary to shoot him down.

And shoot they did.

Marcinko was investigated, then charged with conspiracy to commit financial fraud. He was demoted from captain to commander and sent to jail. And that was the end of SEAL Team Six, sort of. The unit was renamed and a reformer was brought in to "clean things up." Mob Six operators retired or were sent to the regular SEAL teams to spread their knowledge.

While he was in prison, Demo Dick stopped being the quiet professional. He wrote *Rogue Warrior,* which led to a number of other bestselling books. These were wildly entertaining (though I wondered whether our superhero embellished a few details, such as that each member of his team could bench-press 500 pounds). As we used to say: "One 'aw shit' wipes out a thousand attaboys."

I believe that this warrior is not fully appreciated within the SEALs today for his contribution to the community and the country. His legacy is, however. The former SEAL Team Six has produced stunning results since his departure, including high-profile operations such as the rescue of Captain Richard Phillips and the takedown of Osama bin Laden. The culture that Demo Dick fostered, with its intense focus on *curiosity, innovation,* and *simplicity,* has only grown stronger since those inauspicious beginnings. That team strives for excellence every damn day. Let's see how they do it.

CURIOSITY

As we saw with Demo Dick, excellence stems from a deep curiosity that leads one to continuously challenge the status quo. Leaders who strive for excellence are the exact opposite of those mentally organized to protect or take advantage of the status quo. As at SEAL Team Six, there is always friction between the protectors and the curious. This is not to say that the protectors are bad. After all, curiosity can create wildfires if not coupled with discipline and risk management. Those wildfires consume everything in their path if left unchecked. Freewheeling and lawless behavior would reign. It was that line between innovation and recklessness that caused McRaven concern when he was at the command. It is from the heat caused by the friction between these two types of individuals that excellence is created—like a controlled burn done to renew a forest.

That balance is necessary. In fact, if it's not maintained and curiosity is stifled, your business will stagnate. Creativity must be promoted, but as is true with rebuilding an airplane in flight, you've got to keep things moving while the curious tinker.

The curious will never be satisfied and always ask versions of four key questions:

- **Why is this being done this way?**

- **What *should* be done instead?**

- **How can we do it better?**

- **Who is the right person or team to do it?**

The why is the intention, the what is the strategy, the how is the tactics employed, and the who are the operators. To be curious means questioning these four things at all times for anything that is important or that needs to be improved.

It is entirely possible, especially if a great deal of time has passed, that when it comes to stating why something is done, people will have forgotten the reason. The why may no longer be relevant. What's to be done about that? Sometimes nothing. Sometimes everything. Oftentimes, what's being done right now is based upon an old why and is not what needs to be done for the new why. Many teams get lost when their why changes, but the how and the who don't.

The curious aren't satisfied with yesterday's wins or accomplishments, either. They rarely let their guard down on the quest—excellence takes no time off from innovating. Elite teams don't rest on their laurels in the wake of a big success. They will enjoy a brief celebration, learn from the experience, and then move on to the next mission. My favorite sign on the SEAL training tarmac (called the grinder because it is where character is ground down and then rebuilt) states: THE ONLY EASY DAY WAS YESTERDAY.

Yesterday was incredible. Great! Now get over it and get on with things.

Move on, because today is another day. The more common mindset is to celebrate the victories for days on end, and even resist getting back to the deep work—because how could things possibly get any better? So much work had to be done to get that win, surely it's okay to coast a bit. Excellence is always, *always* striving for the next big thing—always growing and exploring.

The curious study the past, looking for echoes of lessons lost. This is a powerful method to gain insight. Marcinko was keenly aware that what was successful in Vietnam wouldn't work the same way against the terrorists. But he didn't shit-can the old tactics entirely. Instead he strove to improve upon them with new technologies and SOPs.

An aphorism often attributed to Mark Twain is appropriate here: "History doesn't repeat itself, but it often rhymes." The curious embraces this notion. Don't pretend you have all the answers. Look to the past to see how a thing was done, then apply a modern context—modern equipment and modern thinking—and see what comes out of that.

You don't always need to reinvent the wheel. Sometimes its better to add or subtract to change the design.

At the turn of the century, my great-grandfather's company made canvas cushion wheels, which are metal wheels with canvas packed around the outside. It made them rock hard, but with just enough padding to absorb some of the impact. A metal wheel would eventually break, but a canvas cushion wheel could last for decades. Henry Ford was a client, using them for the first automobiles. They made for a bumpy ride.

DuPont scientists came along armed with their own curiosity and subtracted the canvas to add rubber. When Ford bought DuPont's tires, it was good for the car owners, but bad for Divine Brothers. Amazingly, Divine canvas wheels from the early 1900s are still used in some Otis elevators today. Some things are built to last.

INNOVATION

Curiosity relates to exploring and expanding one's perspective, and innovation is about using that new perspective to take bold action, creating something new. That means expanding your vision about what is possible and having the courage to do something with that knowledge. In that way innovation is a mindset—being eager for change and doing things differently. It's not assuming that you've got it all figured out, or that your techniques, tools, and procedures are always going to work.

Innovation happens naturally to those who can't help but tinker. An innovator thinks, *I should probably break this and remake it better.* They combine the old with the new through the art of emulation, addition, and subtraction.

For example, the SEALs emulate the Spartans of old, but they modified certain elements. They were not about to use metal armor, swords, and spears while their enemy is using a high-powered rifle. However, they did employ Spartan training methods and philosophies—such as using wrestling to train courage and understand fear; using breathing techniques to develop control of the stress arousal response (sprinting 800 meters in full battle gear with a mouthful of water); and marching long distances with a heavy load to develop durability. These training methods were not invented by the SEALs, but were adapted from those used by the ancient warriors.

The SEALs also bring in ideas from civilian industries that can improve how they engage the enemy. Examples include off-the-shelf technology used for night vision and high-powered flashlights to blind the enemy when entering dark places. SEALs learned the nuances of technical rock climbing from pioneering climbers like Mark Twight. They adopted commercial diving innovations from legends like Jacques Cousteau. Other cool ideas they have picked up on include wingsuit jumping, remotely operated underwater vehicles (ROVs), wave runners, and dune buggies. When the SEALs couldn't buy something they needed, they borrowed or built it. The entire tactical backpack industry was started by my SEAL Team Three teammate Mike Noel. Mike was a parachute rigger who built his own packs; then guys started asking for their own. Soon he had a company, Blackhawk, which has found big success in the civilian adventure gear space.

Innovation requires that you always try to see things from different angles. Take a problem and look at it from the inside out, or reverse-engineer it. Look at a challenge from its end state and work backward, or start in the middle and expand out in both directions. See if you can turn it upside down, or as McRaven would do, break it into its smallest knowable parts and work them separately and sequentially.

Always ask: What are the other ways to solve this problem?

It's important to remember that innovation can be a complete overhaul or it can be incremental, as in a 10 percent improvement. Oftentimes you'll have both. You'll strive for a total change and find only a 10 percent improvement. Other times, you might be looking for nothing more than an incremental change and realize that you got a complete overhaul.

The organizational structure of your company can have a big impact on whether you have a culture of innovation. A centralized, bureaucratic organization is not going to innovate as well as a decentralized, more agile one. When you work in a company that is highly centralized and you're looking to innovate, you almost always have to try the 10 percent approach, because it is exceedingly difficult to achieve a complete overhaul in a large organization with more rigid thinking and significant budgets at risk. However, it does depend on the nature of the organization and the type of innovation you're striving for. Large-scale organizations have managed to innovate by creating protected innovation cultures within skunkworks projects. The Japanese electronics giant Fujitsu is doing this through their Open Innovation Gateway, which we will discuss later in the chapter.

Innovation often comes out of a crisis, when the existential pressure is on. Twitter was running out of money fast and needed fresh thinking. The CEO gave everyone a small budget to try to come up with something new. One of the engineers had the idea to make a microblogging platform. It was cool enough to run with, and it took off. The innovation led to a complete change in the culture and structure of the company. If they had only gone for a 10 percent solution, they would likely no longer be in business. Consider whether you're throwing a Hail Mary to innovate a whole new market segment or if you're just trying to improve how you do business.

If you're not clear about your end state, you can waste a lot of valuable time on innovation. You must deploy a model to vet ideas that simply don't fit. Otherwise you'll find yourself forever chasing the next good idea down a rabbit hole. In *The Way of the SEAL,* I introduced a simple model to help vet new projects. It is called the FITS (fit, importance, timing, simplicity) Model.

Take an idea about an innovation you're considering and put it through the following filter, asking these questions:

- **FIT: Does the innovation fit the team right now in terms of the mission need, the team's capabilities and character, and the energy available to focus on it? Is the risk acceptable?**

■ **IMPORTANCE:** How important is this idea? When you stack it up against your other innovation initiatives, is it in the top three? What is the potential return on investment, and is it worth the time, energy, and resources it will take? What are the consequences if you do *not* take on the project?

■ **TIMING:** Is the timing right for this innovation? Often we jump into something sexy, but we are either too early or too late. It could be too late in that the innovation is now irrelevant and something else is required, or it's too early in that either the technology or your team is not quite ready to develop or exploit it.

■ **SIMPLICITY:** Can we do this simply, or is it going to turn into another ten-tentacled sea monster? If you can't find a simple solution, consider going back to the drawing board.

Elite teams know that the secret lies with the *"in"* in *innovate*. By this I mean that they are aware that innovation is an inside job—that the best ideas come from spontaneous insight, creative expression, reflection, contemplation, and even meditation. It's not always just research and putting pen to paper. There is a great deal of intuitive tinkering involved.

Innovators often have a special place they go to do their creative thinking. This is a private place, a quiet location where they can visualize, contemplate, and ruminate. They may have a mental space they go to (I call this the *mind gym*), an internal visualization where they do the deepest creative work.

Another method for spurring the creative juices is to cultivate a passion for reading and studying about lots of different subjects. I endeavor to read a book a week, at a minimum. This practice is supercharged if you journal or write on subjects that interest you. Over time this knowledge becomes part of your "background of obviousness" and will spontaneously link up with other ideas in your creative sessions. I like to journal ideas every morning—just writing them down in a stream of consciousness. What insights do I have? What can be improved or created? How can I envision getting these things done?

Finally, drawing is another excellent catalyst for creativity. We tend to think differently with pictures, which of course speak a thousand words. If you can draw those pictures, it can be surprisingly useful. You don't have to be an artist—just start drawing. Create an image in your mind, draw it out as best you can, then write some simple words or phrases for details in the margins. Keep an innovation journal. Consider enrolling in a drawing class to open up your creative mind. I recommend the book *Drawing on the Right Side of the Brain* by Betty Edwards, as well as the workshops based on this book. Be like Leonardo and use drawings to express your internal inventor.

SIMPLICITY

Less is more. You want to keep things as simple as possible—but you know that simple is not easy. In fact, achieving simplicity is the opposite of easy. Our brains tend to complicate things. We can get caught up in our own brilliant ideas and mistake more features for better. If you can take a thousand words and distill them down into a short, clear paragraph, that is a sign of mastery. Getting to simplicity requires patience and practice.

Marcinko understood simplicity. He appreciated that in order to truly succeed in his world, he had to narrow the team's focus and specialize. He didn't want the SEALs under his command to train to do everything under the sun, like the other teams were doing. He identified the narrow range of skills they would need to master. They then relentlessly trained those tactics, such as insertion and extraction from different platforms, including parachuting, diving, and mobility. They also trained to be the best shooters in the world, especially in close quarter combat.

He also simplified the team's operating rhythm. At the other SEAL teams, the operating units trained for twelve months or longer, and then deployed for six. He thought this was cumbersome and kept the men away from their families for too long. So he created a "four on, four off" cycle. For four months, the men would be deployed, then for the next four months, they would be in training mode, operating from their base on the East Coast. This gave them more time to spend with their families and to further their education and pursue other interests, like a martial art. This model helped the force remain healthier and more balanced and focused on the job. He was way before his time in understanding what made his operators effective in body, mind, and spirit. However, even when they were in the home-time mode, the units had to be ready to go at a moment's notice. They were required to keep their go bags nearby and carry a pager—ready to board the helo within six hours of that beep.

THE MEANING OF LIFE IS SIMPLE

There is a fun story I like to tell about simplicity.

Once upon a time there was a benevolent ruler who wanted to know if there was a meaning to life that he was missing. So he sent his wise men out to study all the world's knowledge, giving them a year to accomplish this enormous feat. At the end of that year, they returned triumphantly with seventeen volumes containing all of the knowledge known to mankind. Within those volumes was the secret.

The king was pleased but said to them: "This is great, guys, but I don't have the time to actually read all of this. Can you reduce it to just one volume?"

The wise men advised him that of course this was impossible. There was simply too much knowledge.

"Then it's off with your heads," the king replied. Hearing that, the wise men quickly agreed to reduce it to one volume. The king gave them six months.

Half a year later, the men returned, and explained that after much gnashing of teeth and scratching of heads, they had simplified all the knowledge into one volume. They gave it to the king, who was pleased.

"This is really quite good. In fact, it's too valuable for only us at the top to know," the king said. "The other leaders in the kingdom need this knowledge, and I'm afraid that as it stands now, it might be over their heads. Let's reduce it to one chapter!"

The wise men threw up their hands in despair. The king reminded them that their lives depended on completing this task. This time they had three months to make the complex simple.

Against all odds, the men once again accomplished the impossible. They handed the result to the king. He approved it and ordered it to be disseminated to the leaders within the kingdom. They reported back that the information was indeed incredible, and wished to share it with those under their rule.

The king asked to reduce it now to a single paragraph.

The wearied men produced once again. All of the literate subjects read the paragraph and declared loudly that *everyone* needed this knowledge. So the king had it reduced to a single phrase.

"This is it!" the king shouted. "You've done it. Speak it loudly from the ramparts! Everyone in the kingdom must know the meaning of life."

What was written on that slip of paper? This is heavy stuff. It might change your life.

The paper read . . . drumroll, please . . . *There ain't no such thing as a free lunch.*

This story is a fun way of discussing just how much work getting to simplicity can be. But it is doable, and definitely worth the effort.

Imagine the difficulty in taking seventeen volumes of text and reducing it to one sentence. It's almost like taking all of the buttons and features on a phone and condensing them to one home button.

Sound familiar?

Ask yourself: Can I describe what I'm going to do in a short paragraph, or even in one sentence? If you can't, then you've got work to do. Always determine what you can cut out.

In order to think with simplicity, you have to begin to live with simplicity. Someone with a complicated life would have a great deal of difficulty doing this. The men of SEAL Team Six were minimalists. They didn't own a lot of material things. They were willing to walk away from what they had at a moment's notice, and they often did.

I also did so on numerous occasions—just grabbed my go bag and off I was to the next adventure. It's harder to do now with a family in tow. When I left New York to join the SEALs, the only thing I had were the clothes on my back and the martial arts training weapon called a bo staff—an item that wasn't very useful in my new job. In fact, when I stepped off the bus at Officer Candidate School, a large stick in my hand, the top-hatted instructor's face lit up as he stated he knew exactly where I could store it. Later, when I left SEAL Team Three for SEAL Delivery Vehicle Team One in Hawaii, the Navy shipped everything I owned to me. It wasn't much. I had already sold my house and motorcycle, and I left much of my furniture behind. Then my new rental in Hawaii was so small that I didn't have room for over half of what I had shipped over, so I gave most of it to the movers on the spot. I was practicing an important rule of simplicity: travel light and don't get attached to your stuff. Truthfully, it was quite liberating to walk away from all of that junk.

Always ask yourself what you can let go of, both material possessions and also projects or commitments you have taken on. This will free up mental space for your innovation muscles. The way you can frame this is to always ask yourself what you can let go of to keep things simple. This question serves as a filter to keep time and energy available to innovate.

Simplicity also means disciplining yourself to avoid time sucks and endless distractions. One of the reasons I don't go to the office more than twice a week now is because I get pulled into conversations left and right. I don't mean that having these discussions is a negative thing—I need to be out in the field, as we will see later with the principle of alignment—but it's also easy to get an hour or more sucked out of your day unintentionally. Socializing with your team is important, but it can get in the way when you need to do the deep, creative work.

Much has been written about the attention and time suck from undisciplined use of digital devices and social media. Cal Newport's book *Digital Minimalism* outlines ways to deny these distractions their power. Jumping from one hack to another to try to optimize your life can be another time suck—no fad diet, new brain-training app, or intense breathing technique is going to help you stare down the fear wolf. Better to stick with a time-tested developmental method and do the work daily until you transform yourself. Bouncing around like a jumping bean drains your energy and keeps you distracted.

I can't emphasize enough how powerful this principle is. Commit now to simplify things and get really clear about what's important and what's not. When you reach that level of clarity—where you're aware of what your immediate mission is moment to moment, things start to really take off. Here are some focusing questions I use myself to keep things simple:

Is what am I doing right now (or about to do) in alignment with my (or ours if a team) mission?

What's the most important thing I can focus on right now—that will move me toward mission accomplishment?

Does this idea or new project pass the FITS test?

Can I say no to this in service to a higher yes?

Is this process worthy of breaking to improve?

I also employ Dwight Eisenhower's exceptional planning matrix to make sure that what I have chosen to focus on is important, not just urgent. The matrix has you consider the urgency and importance of your tasks and projects. You endeavor to focus only on those that fall into categories 1 and 2 below. The rest you delegate or let go of.

THE EISENHOWER DECISION MATRIX

1. It is urgent AND important.

2. It is NOT urgent, BUT it is important.

3. It is urgent and NOT important.

4. It is NOT urgent and NOT important.

TRAIN YOUR CONCENTRATION

Teams who train their concentration together have a better capacity to radically simplify and focus to drive excellence. What does this training look like? My team performs box breathing together for five minutes before *every* meeting, including virtual calls. This technique is both simple and very effective. Box breathing doubles as a concentration and stress management tool when you focus on the breathing pattern. So the team gets to work on their arousal control and attention control a few times a day. If five minutes seems too much, then just one minute is a good starting point. I recently taught this to the international executive team at Walmart, who were looking for innovative ideas to deal with their own constant crush of stress. It is great to see interest in these practices finally coming from the C-suites.

Concentration has four elements, the first of which is the intention to focus on something useful and important. This refers to the outcome you seek in terms of what you want or need to focus on. These are the things that pass the FITS test and are in categories 1 and 2 of the Eisenhower matrix. You must get clear about what your intentions are in order to execute with concentrated excellence.

Controlling one's attention while focusing on the object of intention is the second element. If we use the metaphor of driving, if the intention is the destination, then attention control is steering down the right road that will get you to that destination.

But that's still not enough.

The third skill is to develop concentrated staying power so you don't drive off the road or into another car. It's easy to get distracted time and again, meaning you get nowhere fast. Staying power is your cruise control, your ability to keep your attention on your desired object and moving steadily toward your destination for long periods of deep work.

Finally, concentration requires periodic rests to recover and refuel. Concentrating on your most worthy goals and innovative projects is hard work—you need to take a break every now and again. Then when you reengage and step on the gas again you will have more energy and willpower.

In other words, train yourself to focus *and* to not burn out.

One practice I use for recovery is what I call a *circle day*. It's an idea I got from Buddhist businessman Geshe Michael Roach from his book *The Diamond Cutter*. Draw a circle around days you intend to do deep, intensive work calling for concentration—creating, writing, planning, as well as recovery. Then protect that time with a vengeance, even doing the work at a place different from where you normally operate, such as your home, a co-work space, or a coffee shop. I don't allow any phone calls, meetings, or other distractions to happen during this time. I turn my phone off and put it in the bottom of my backpack.

You can do this for short or long blocks of time. I circled weeks to work on this book in Utah and Hawaii as writing retreats (and for some great r & r). I circle two days every week for deep work and don't miss those unless I am using that week for some other creative work, such as recording podcasts or my coaching events.

Some people find it useful to circle the first few hours of their day for creative work. You yourself have to figure out what schedule suits you best. Every creative person who produces a lot of good work has his or her take on this. Cal Newport discusses these creative habits in detail in *Deep Work*. Whatever works for you is the right plan. At your company, consider that big open work spaces can cause loss of focus. Help your team protect their time by having mandated circle times with no phone calls or social media usage— just complete silence for deep work. Company retreats are a useful method for deep work if you build in the time. Consider having a digital diet of checking email, texts, Slack, and other social media only at lunch and the end of the day to allow minds to settle and go deeper.

THE BUSHIDO WAY

I've been invited to work with the Japanese company Fujitsu for several years now. Fujitsu is a $50 billion electronics and engineering company that's been described as the IBM of Japan. The company is a bureaucratic monster, but management recognizes that VUCA is pushing them to be curious and to evolve. The unit I have worked with is a special entrepreneurial development unit called the Open Innovation Gateway (OIG) located in Silicon Valley.

Mohi Ahmed launched the OIG to bring best practices of entrepreneurship into Fujitsu. Ahmed had to get curious about how Fujitsu could improve—how they could develop leaders comfortable in VUCA.

There is a cultural bias, a fear wolf pattern in the Japanese culture around not speaking out in order to maintain the status quo. They call it *saving face*. As a result, entrepreneurship, which is all about breaking with the status quo, does not come naturally to them. But they can train to overcome this bias. Mohi appreciates that developing entrepreneurial leaders in the bureaucratic culture can be challenging. He seeks out the young leaders in the organization with that potential and teaches them how to be more curious and innovative—how to develop simpler solutions to complex challenges.

Ahmed looked at existing cultures of innovation such as Google Labs, Lockheed Martin's Skunk Works, the venture capital community's incubators, and also the Navy SEALs. He drew out their best practices to support the OIG. He employed the concept of emulation, molding what he has learned to fit the Fujitsu culture.

He also leveraged Japan's warrior legacy.

As the SEALs used the Spartans for inspiration, Mohi sought inspiration from the fabled Japanese Samurai. Excellence, innovation, and simplicity are baked into the Samurai code of conduct, called the Bushido code. Samurai warriors emphasized the beginner's mind, which I experienced through my own Zen training. This involves emptying your cup so you can always be learning, not stuck in rigid beliefs and ideas on how to do things. That ethos fosters flexibility and curiosity, which of course leads to innovation.

Ahmed embraced these ideas and has built them into a code of conduct at OIG. And when it came to simplicity, he decided to keep his organization small and nimble, with a staff of fewer than four individuals. The vision is also simple and clear. Here Mohi articulates the vision of his special mission unit:

At Open Innovation Gateway (OIG), we are focused on
Innovation with a purpose. We call this approach "wise

innovation." *We want to help our customers and partners innovate not only faster, but also wiser. Excellence is key to our processes. Such excellence doesn't merely mean doing a good job, or even a great job. It means going well beyond what is expected. In our team, excellence means that the scope of what is possible has been expanded. The key to open innovation is having an open mind. That sounds easy and yet can take a lifetime to fully understand. An open mind requires acknowledgment of the limitations of our knowledge and skill—but not in the negative sense. Only through maintaining humility can we look beyond what we think we know and accept new ideas.*

While openness punches holes in the box, we seek to think outside it. That takes curiosity. Curiosity is the motivating force behind new understanding. It pushes us to explore new lands, both literally and metaphorically. At OIG, we find power in our curiosity. We can explore new ideas and co-create new possibilities with others. Curiosity takes us to the new and unexplored territories where innovation can flourish. "I always wondered about . . ." "Is there anything vaguely similar to . . ." "I wonder what would happen if . . ." These are the language cues of innovation.

That kind of thinking provides the spark for innovation at OIG, but those sparks can get smothered pretty easily.

Adding complexity obscures the initial vision of the innovation.

New features, an attempt to be all things to all people, even byzantine corporate processes can kill excellence. There needs to be a ruthless drive for simplicity as well.

Maintaining simplicity is harder than it may seem. Any new idea, product, service, way of thinking—even a new commitment—inherently doesn't fit into the existing structures and processes. The mismatch is why it was hard to conceive of before. The mismatch is an inevitable function of thinking and being outside the box. It's common to try to force the new thing into the existing framework. Layers of adapters are added to make the new feel a bit more like the old. Doing this obscures the beauty and simplicity of the new—and often destroys it.

Simplicity isn't merely about making an innovation easier to execute. It is about maintaining the dignity and integrity of innovation, about keeping it pure and testable. This is a critical point. Just because something is new doesn't mean it is good. It needs to be tested.

At OIG, they test every single idea by embodying them in simple prototypes. Then they test the prototypes with actual customers who would benefit from the ideas. The ideas may help OIG's customers solve problems. But if the idea embodied in the prototype is buried under layers of complexity, then when they test it for market acceptance, the feedback they get is about the complexity that surrounds the innovation, not the simple essence of the idea. For OIG, simplicity isn't an option, but a requirement in everything they do.

OIG's logo is a Zen calligraphy circle, with each brushstroke of that circle related to their mission. It's quite profound.

Mohi brought me in to share my ideas with his elite team, yet I was equally rewarded with valuable insight into how a different culture approaches excellence. I saw that curiosity and innovation don't happen without simplicity—it is a bedrock principle. We have so much to learn from other cultures!

About the OIG Logo

The logo is a variation on a traditional Japanese brush painted form known as an "Enso." This rendering was created for the Open Innovation Gateway (OIG) by Tango Matsumoto.

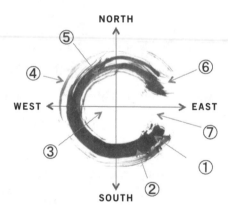

①   BEGINNING OF THE JOURNEY: **Start with confidence and optimism**

②   NOBLE-PURPLE: **Aspire to a higher state of mind**

③   EMPTY SPACE: **Embrace new possibilities with purity**

④   MANY LINES: **Engage individuals to drive unified action**

⑤   VARIED SHAPES: **Energize community through dynamic non-uniformity**

⑥   ENDING STROKE: **Open oneself to the unknown, inside-out, outside-in**

⑦   OPENING ON THE RIGHT: **Face the sunrise—begin a new journey**

SWIMMING WITH SHARKS

When I was in Iraq with SEAL Team One, I decided that when I returned to the States I would leave my PhD and adjunct professor role to radically focus on my business. I wanted to pivot NavySEALS.com away from online sales and to training mental toughness, leadership, and teamwork. Out of that decision, I bid on and won a government contract to form a nationwide mentoring program for Navy SEAL candidates. The Navy needed to increase the number of SEALs. One way to do that, they believed, was to improve the quality of the candidates who walked in the front door. This would increase the throughput at BUD/S later on—which it did by approximately 5 percent over time.

My company was hired as a subcontractor by a prime contractor to design, launch, and manage the initiative—called the Naval Special Warfare Mentor Program. I designed it and put together a plan to hire thirty-six former SEALs, placing them at recruiting districts to work with the special ops candidates. This new team got busy right away preparing the next generation of Navy SEALs.

Within a year of the five-year contract, the team had greatly exceeded the expectations of the end client, the Navy Recruiting Command. It was also when I lost the contract to the powerful billion-dollar Blackwater USA, owned by another Navy SEAL. I was told later that he thought his company should have won the original contract—an upstart organization like mine had no business swimming in the same (shark-infested) waters as his Blackwater.

The world of government contracting was a big unknown for me, and I quickly learned that it is ruthless. Blackwater challenged the prime contractor, asserting they had outgrown their small business status. The prime contractor lost that challenge, and then I lost the contract. Blackwater and its leader had mastered the game of influence, and I was the small fish who got eaten by the shark.

Some advisors thought there may be fraud involved, and that I should fight back. Because I was committed to my meditation and emotional development, I used those skills to aide my decision-making. I wanted to avoid the type of fear-based reactionary thinking that hadn't worked out so well in the past. So I went back to the Zen bench to contemplate a way forward. After a few days, I got the strong intuitive sense that it wouldn't serve me in the long run to fight Blackwater. Not only that, but I should get out of government contracting altogether. The negative aspects of such work meant it just was not for me. My sense was that I would be more innovative and have a bigger impact in the commercial sector.

Within three months of losing that $10 million contract, I had rebranded my company as SEALFIT. There I would train SEAL and other special ops candidates in a way that I could never do within the former bureaucratic constraints. I would focus on developing the candidates not just physically, but along a broader spectrum of leadership and team character. I envisioned incorporating some tools that'd had a dramatic impact on my own development—from Zen and the martial arts to yoga, as well as human performance and other mental and emotional training methods. These methods are not formally taught to SEALs.

I was taking inspiration from innovators like Marcinko and learning from my earlier disasters. By the time I launched SEALFIT in 2007, I was able to implement most of the commitments discussed in this book. I needed to employ everything I had learned, and to become a voracious student of the human potential and development worlds, all things physical, mental, emotional, intuitional, and spiritual.

My first product was a live-in academy based on the way the Spartans and Shaolin monks would have trained. Special ops students lived at my training center in Encinitas, California, for thirty days at a time—a total immersive experience. They trained from six A.M. until ten P.M. daily, sometimes around the clock. I ran these events four times a year for several years, and they were a huge success. The SEALs and other special forces candidates who attended were sailing through their respective training programs, and outsiders looking in started to take note. But personally I started to burn out as the other demands of the business required equal attention. I needed to find a way to replicate myself to scale things, and more important, to rebalance my life.

In other words, as things got more complicated, I felt the intuitive pull to simplify again.

That meant I had to innovate a sustainable and scalable business model—one not so dependent on me. I decided to train and certify coaches in my methods. That required that I simplify and clarify the teachings. That academy is now taught in a series of shorter, progressively more challenging events, all by certified coaches. These coaches then track and guide progress as the students continue their developmental journey.

Based on my success training the special ops men and women, I was asked by many entrepreneurs and executives to bring the training to their world. I did not want to dilute the experience, so instead I chose to innovate again by translating the principles and tools for this new audience, which became a bestselling book titled *Unbeatable Mind* and the integrated vertical development program by that same name. I was utilizing the same principles that Demo Dick did to constantly evolve the team and simplify the mission to meet the evolving VUCA world. Ten years after I had lost that government contract, my business was thriving and serving not one customer—the U.S. government— but thousands of SOF operators, entrepreneurs, and executives, along with many sports and corporate teams. It has been a constant churn of innovation as we strive for our own version of excellence.

But I certainly wasn't done with my journey of staring down the wolf. VUCA has a way of putting the best ideas and business models to the test. I was about to learn that my business's resiliency was related to my own as a leader. Let's look at how this sixth commitment of resiliency will ensure your durability in business and life.

SDTW Exercise 6:
CURIOSITY, INNOVATION, AND SIMPLICITY

Prepare your mind as with the previous exercises, then begin planning to upgrade your excellence with the following drills:

1. Get curious about something new that will challenge your brain to expand its creativity muscles. Make a list of things you are interested in learning, or are passionate about, and want to explore (such as writing, drawing, singing, art, acting, improv, etc.). Then put them through the FITS model to cull the list down to one item that fits you now. Now plan how you will go deep into this new thing: start a class, find a mentor, buy a book, etc.

2. Journal to innovate. Begin to write down five new ideas every morning after your morning ritual. These can be unrelated ideas or can fit within a single concept you are trying to innovate, evolve, or create. Consider looking at the issue from multiple perspectives: inside out, backward, upside down, from another dimension altogether (for example, matter to fluid to space, or biology versus electronic, etc.).

3. Keep it Simple, Sally. What can you cut out, eliminate, sell, donate, or off-load? Start with material things, then move to commitments and even people who drag you down. Finally, consider limiting beliefs. Stare down the fear wolf and KISS things!

LEADERSHIP
COMMITMENT
#6

COMMIT TO
RESILIENCY

STARE DOWN THE FEAR OF OBSTACLES

Marcus Luttrell was born in Houston, Texas, alongside a twin

brother. Both were rough-and-tumble kids who decided at an

early age that they wanted to be part of the legendary SEAL

Teams. At age fourteen, they found a mentor to help. Every

week, for four years, they trained their bodies and minds to

become the type of men worthy of the Navy SEALs. Through

this dedicated focus, Marcus already displayed many of the aspects of resiliency required to be a team guy. The brothers enlisted in the Navy at eighteen and shortly reported to BUD/S Class 226.

Marcus fell off the obstacle course early in training, fracturing his femur. For most this would have been game over—but he soldiered on. After the bone healed, he was allowed to start again with Class 228, from which he graduated nine months later. Over two years of training to earn the trident.

Easy day.

Marcus's first combat deployment was to Iraq. While there, he soaked up knowledge and experience, paying close attention to the seasoned operators. To earn the respect and trust of his team, he worked hard, kept his mouth shut and eyes open. He had seen that reputation is the primary currency in the SEALs. Are you a good operator or not? Do you earn your trident every day? The SEALs knew that you could focus on operational and tactical skills and still be a Grade A jerk. Therefore, the best leaders look for both skills and character before they give you the respect of an operator. Marcus soon gained a solid reputation for both.

When presented with a challenge, such as fracturing his leg, he responded in a way that made him stronger and better. This chapter is about resiliency, which is the ability to become a better person *because* of the obstacles we face in life, not in spite of them. Ryan Holiday says that *The Obstacle Is the Way* in his book by that title. I agree, and so do many SEAL leaders. The obstacles become your way to evolve your character and become a better person all around.

Marcus Luttrell would find many obstacles during his time in the teams. He would prove his resiliency, time and again.

In 2005, Luttrell was deployed to Afghanistan as the senior enlisted leader on a four-person recon team in Operation Red Wings. The mission was to identify the whereabouts of, and if possible to capture, a senior level insurgent. He and his three teammates were dropped deep into the rugged mountains.

The insurgents were holed up in a small village in a valley surrounded by steep and gnarly terrain. This was their base of operations, whether the locals liked it or not. Luttrell and his team were inserted some distance away from the village, performing a foot patrol to set up an observation post.

The op was proceeding as planned when without warning, a pair of teenage goatherds stumbled upon the four-man team. The SEALs were not close enough to restrain the teenagers, yet knew that they would inform the insurgents. The moral dilemma: Should they prevent them from reporting their location (by killing them), or let them go and hope for the best? The teens were unarmed noncombatants, and it was against the Geneva Conventions and U.S. military protocols to harm unarmed civilians. However, in this strange war, even kids were put in the position of combatants, and the team considered that possibility. Some would question their actions back home if they took the kids out, but many would argue that preserving the mission, and their lives, was the right move.

Ticktock, ticktock.

While the team pondered these thoughts, the kids turned tail and bolted down the mountain like billy goats. The SEALs were too loaded down and out of their element to give effective chase. There was no way to stop them now. Luttrell and his teammates let them go.

It was a fateful decision.

The op was compromised. They moved as fast as possible to their extraction point. Soon they were flanked by the enemy from three sides on the mountain. Heavy machine gunfire and RPG rocket, screamed at them. Mortars whistled inbound. This was a serious shit storm, with the four SEALs facing a much larger force in better fighting positions. The only advantage they had was their vastly superior training. It was that training that saved Luttrell.

It did not save his teammates.

The mission leader, Lieutenant Michael Murphy, tried to call for the QRF backup. Because the team was surrounded on all sides by the mountains, he couldn't get through on his radio. They would need to fight their way out without support. Darkness was setting in, complicating matters further.

In an act of desperation, Murphy sprinted to higher ground to use his sat phone to make the call. This exposed him to direct enemy fire, which he fully knew would be the case. He sacrificed himself to give his team a chance. Lieutenant Murphy was shot, and shortly thereafter, SEALs Danny Dietz and Matthew Axelson also went down. The QRF was inbound, and tragically the helicopter was hit with a rocket as it approached, killing all aboard. The op went from seriously bad to a complete disaster.

Luttrell was reeling from the loss of his team, fighting for his life. He was literally shot off the mountain into a ravine, tumbling and rolling. Rocks and other debris were blasted in all directions and he was knocked unconscious as a rocket exploded nearby. When he revived, it was pitch-dark and eerily silent. By the grace of God, the enemy hadn't found him. They probably assumed that they'd killed all four and could come back to recover the bodies in daylight. Luttrell was injured, though not mortally, and made his way down the mountain in the hopes of finding a more welcoming place.

He ran into a civilian from the Pashtun village. The tribal custom is that if they find someone in need and offer help, then they are bound to protect their charge with their lives. This villager decided to help Luttrell at great risk to himself and his family. He escorted Luttrell to the village and hid him from the insurgents. The man then found a way to alert American forces that he was hiding an injured U.S. soldier. A few days later, a detachment of Army Rangers recovered Luttrell, though they also ended up in a firefight with the same group, which was by then going door to door looking for Luttrell.

The film *Lone Survivor* is based on Luttrell's account of this incident. There were several days back in Coronado when we received reports that Luttrell had been captured. That was a shocker, since no SEAL had ever been captured. When he turned up alive later, it was a genuine "holy shit" moment of relief, interrupting the sadness for the loss of the other great men.

Luttrell struggled with his physical and emotional wounds.

The service wanted to medically retire him—but he pushed back hard, saying he wasn't done yet. He wanted to be with his teammates. That was how he would recover and use his innate resiliency to move on.

The service agreed, and eventually he was back into the fight again, this time with SEAL Team Five in the hot spot of Ramadi, Iraq. There Luttrell injured his liver and fractured his spine. Finally, and still against his will, he was medically retired. If it had been up to him, he'd still be fighting to this day.

Marcus's whole life since has been in honor of the teammates he lost on that mountaintop. He wrote the book, acted in the movie, and launched the Lone Survivor Foundation to tell their story and support the families of fallen heroes.

At every stage of his journey, this resilient warrior responded positively and wouldn't quit, no matter the circumstances. His mindset was to constantly move forward; any time he fell down, he got up stronger than before. He exemplified the three traits of resiliency worthy of deeper discussion: *adaptability, persistence,* and *learning.* Let's look into them now.

ADAPTABILITY

Zen master Nakamura scribbled on the chalkboard, the screeching sound setting my teeth on edge. The words were written in Japanese kanji characters. Beneath these, he translated for us before we could ask: "Fall down seven times, get up eight." He then gave a beautiful account of the meaning in his broken English. What he conveyed was way more nuanced than the words alone implied. The main point he made was not just that you should get up after falling down, but that what counts is how well you get up.

How often have you "fallen down" in life and reacted poorly, or risen with timidity, not adapting quickly to the new reality? I used to do that. And it is the more common reaction. We say to ourselves: *Holy shit, where did that come from? Why me?* And it appears that others revel in your disaster, happy to see you on your ass, glad that it wasn't them and thinking maybe your fall will spare them. Or more likely, people like to see you fail because it makes them feel better about their own fallibilities.

Reacting negatively to failure leads to more destabilization, worsening an already bad situation. Sometimes it takes years before you can look back and say you're glad it happened, that you see now how it made you stronger and wiser.

That's okay, but it's not how the resilient respond. The resilient stare down their fear of falling off an obstacle and train to get back up right away with a positive response. Like Luttrell, they look for opportunity to turn lemons into lemonade. Fall down seven times, get up eight—stronger, better, and more capable, having learned everything possible from the situation.

That's adaptability.

ELASTICITY

But how does one become adaptable? One way is to practice elasticity—where you stretch and contract repeatedly. And you recover quickly when stretched too far. You must learn to be like a rubber band, expanding and contracting but getting stronger each time instead of weaker.

As an example, Luttrell stretched himself far in BUD/S training and injured himself, but he recovered quickly and graduated soon enough. He had to go back and start all over again, but he did it, stretching to adapt to his new reality. The ability to snap back quickly requires an awareness of how far you can be stretched without breaking permanently. As McRaven taught his team, you must search for the red lines, where the danger zones are, where being overstretched could lead to a serious breakdown. Resilient people are aware of these boundaries and move toward them to explore the territory. Then when something does go wrong, they don't play the victim. They take total responsibility, learn from their mistakes, and get back on track ASAP. They are constantly probing for a new acceptable boundary, where they can fail a little bit, learn from the situation, and then reset the line again for the next test.

This is a practice of balancing effort and release, push and pull, yang and yin. You get pulled in one direction by the marketplace, then in another by your competition, and then in yet another direction by your organization. You're getting stretched in this VUCA world. The question becomes: Can you stretch to learn, fail gracefully, and snap back to recover quickly? How valuable would it be to train that level of elasticity into yourself and your team?

Elasticity is *not* about long-term persistence. It's a daily practice of finding and riding that boundary line just slightly outside your capability and capacity and then pulling back every so often to rebalance. You don't want to pop like a broken rubber band. You stretch a little farther each time—and when you recover, you come back stronger.

PLIANCY

Related to elasticity is pliancy—the ability to change and morph as the challenges hit you rapid fire. In the SEALs we coined the term *Semper Gumby,* which meant always flexible. This was a nod to our Marine brothers, whose motto is *Semper Fi*—always faithful. SEALs are a bit countercultural in the military, and we thought the little green bendy toy Gumby was a pliable mascot. I mean, you could contort it to do all sorts of things, but it always came back to its normal shape with a little effort. Most days I felt like that.

Luttrell has fought his entire life, semper Gumby style, constantly adapting, morphing, and changing to get to his objective. At one point SEALs will be operating in a desert urban environment; the next year they could find themselves in the frigid mountains of Afghanistan in the dead of winter; months after that, they might be in the middle of the Indian Ocean. Your life and career may not seem too different from that, right?

Getting comfortably pliant will allow you to be like Gumby—able to quickly morph and change.

DURABILITY

On the other end of the spectrum is durability. This principle is about pressing on in spite of things breaking down. Certainly we want to be difficult to break and can train our body and mind to be tough, but life sometimes gets in the way of our best intentions. So you and your team also need to be effective when something important is taken offline.

You might have a key project leader or subject matter expert who leaves for another firm or becomes ill or goes on family leave or whatever. You can't have the entire team grind to a halt as a result. You've got to fill the gap quickly and move forward. In the SEALs we built redundancy into our teams and equipment. We expected gear to get lost or damaged on an op, and though we trained hard to avoid it, we were also prepared to continue the mission if a teammate was injured or killed. Durability is a "two is one, one is none" principle. We always had a backup—backup gear, backup skills, and backup plans.

Durability like this is critical for corporate teams in this VUCA world, and it also has both a hard and a soft side to it. Your team should stand strong against the elements, projecting power like the mighty oak. But simultaneously you can bend with the supple softness of a reed, moving with the winds of change. The reed will survive a serious storm, whereas the oak tree can be uprooted.

ATTITUDE

At SEALFIT we relentlessly train those big four skills mentioned earlier: arousal control through the breath; attention control through concentration, visualization, and micro-goals. But no matter how much you practice, if you have a negative attitude, you are toast. Developing control is the first half of the battle, while staring down fear to feed courage is the other half. Negativity allowed in one individual destroys the performance of the entire team.

You must feed the courage wolf. Attitude is more than a platitude—it is an important training tool. The threat that negative thinking and negative emotional energy present you as a leader is a clear and present danger. The team must commit to feeding that courage wolf with positive dialogue and emotional energy to unlock the potential held back by the negative forces.

Does your team have an attitude of "will do"? Or is there a "maybe" or "not sure" lurking beneath the surface? Is the culture upbeat, positive, and mutually supportive, where everyone's win is a win for the team, or are there competitive "I win, you lose" or "I got mine, you're on your own" attitudes? They must stare down that fear of losing and falling down when the obstacles come. Your team's win is your win.

I have seen many teams that purport to be high-performance teams undercut by negative attitudes. This can come from a hypercompetitive third plateau bias. Staunch individualism and competitiveness remain pervasive in Western business culture and are negative in many ways. As you have undoubtedly experienced, it takes only one egocentric, negative individual to crush a team's spirit. That one bad apple will spoil the bunch. Dealing with negative teammates is a real challenge. Let's start by ensuring that we are not that negative apple, then look to the team.

A negative cultural mindset can show up in many ways. The following list is by no means complete:

- Competition where the loser is made to feel like a loser. The reaction is like the loser failed, or is not good enough. It takes some work to foster competition that is growth inducing. I call that *coopetition.*

- Any form of gossip or talk about a team member behind that individual's back.

- Fear-mongering, catastrophizing, and lamenting failures.

- Autocratic leadership, or any leader dominating the culture and conversation.

- Allowing any teammate to be negative, casting doubt, shame, blame, or guilt upon another, or on the team at large.

- Language that includes words like *could have, would have, should have, meant to,* or *can't.*

■ **A low-energy or depressed feeling in the work space. This was something I noticed in the bureaucratic spaces of the military, and dare I say, the DMV.**

Regarding that last bullet, big bureaucratic organizations often have negative environments, incorporating many of the qualities pointed to here. That doesn't mean that all the individuals in such an environment are negative. If you are in one of those organizations, please don't take this personally. This is not meant to be anything but a notice that to perform at your very best, as a leader and a team, you must address this issue inside yourself first, and then with the team.

In the SOF community the best leaders demand a positive mindset. Any individual that somehow slips through training with a negative mindset is made aware of the impact he or she has and is compelled to change—or is asked to leave. Trust and respect are diminished in the presence of negativity.

A positive mindset and emotional state are crucial for adaptability. After all, it is easy to be all rainbows and roses when things are going well. "Everyone wants to be a frogman on a sunny day," was how the SEAL instructors put it. But bring on the shit and let's see how attitude changes, shall we? The power of optimism and a positive mindset cannot be understated.

Research has shown that humans are hardwired for negativity. This is called the negativity bias. Everything "out there" seems negative—the news media and many TV shows and movies are caustic and sarcastic. Yes, they are indeed funny, but watching negative humor will deepen the neural pathways of negative thinking and feeling. At a national level, this has created a dark attitude, which is expressing itself in extreme ways.

You need to push back against negativity, and hard.

Optimism and compassion are outcomes of feeding the courage wolf. The attitude is one of always finding the lessons in our failures and crises—the silver lining. Is your glass half full or half empty? Optimism about the future and the team's capacity to meet its mission, regardless of what is thrown at you, is crucial. As a team, you will find a way—period. You believe that there's always a solution, and when the VUCA winds blow, that, too, will pass. Elite teams have a persistent optimism that they express with positive sayings, similar to all the ones I have been using in these pages. When the inevitable crisis hits, the elite team responds with "We've got this. Easy day, hooyah!" Translated, this means: Good, we needed to learn this lesson. Now we will move forward with more clarity and durability.

This attitude adjustment is another daily practice that requires attention to, and refinement of, your internal dialogue and emotional states.

IT'S ABOUT THE TEAM

A sincere and positive focus on supporting the goals and needs of your teammates is another method to build resiliency. There are two ways to look at this. The first and best is to genuinely care about and take care of the well-being of your teammates.

Unfortunately, in my experience, this is rare; people can be really self-absorbed. That brings me to the second way: Enforce it culturally. In the SEALs, we insisted that each of us check on our swim buddy's gear to make sure it was squared away before and after an op. We would ask what we could do to help and then provide assistance. Then when we were certain he or she was good to go, we turned our attention to our own gear, and our buddy helped us. And even before that, we ensured that the common team gear was dialed in. Thus the pecking order is team first, teammate second, and you last. When this practice is instilled in your group, soon the team is taking care of your gear, asking how they can help you, and making your life easier. When your entire team has your back like this, and you have theirs, you tap into maximum leverage. This becomes a habit, and as the team experiences the mutual benefit, they are less likely to go back to self-serving behavior. You are then not doing it for the transactional intent, but because it is who you are as a person.

Helping others cultivates trust, respect, and goodwill.

This is a powerful practice that requires a shift in perspective from "me first" to "we and then me." It has enormous benefit for the team's performance, as you know you have your teammate's support. We would routinely look our teammates in the eye and state with sincerity: "I've got your back." This reinforced a great sense of unity and mutual care. How many of your teammates do you know, beyond a shadow of doubt, have your back? And you theirs? This is a good test of a team's adaptability.

When you're focused on others—serving them with an attitude of "we're in this together" and "my suffering isn't any greater than your suffering" and "what's good for the team is good for me"—the entire team benefits from the energy and optimism. This creates a virtuous feedback loop where everyone is experiencing deeper trust, respect, and care.

HUMOR

I recommend you use positive humor to help with the really hard situations. I have seen firsthand how you can cultivate this attitude. The best teams find humor in the most miserable situations to get the positive energy flowing again. Laughter truly is effective medicine, and it's free. The oxygen and positivity that flow in when you laugh pack a powerful one-two punch.

I didn't come into the SEALs with a great approach to humor. The humor of my youth was mostly sarcasm—negative and biting. I had to take cues from my teammates to use humor positively. Eventually I could hold my own with the funniest when shit went down. The individual who utilizes humor well knows that it has a profound effect on more than just the team. You leave a carbon copy of the positive energy on yourself.

In some first, second, and third plateau cultures, humor can veer toward the inappropriate. Be aware of this possibility and promote positive humor rather than sarcasm or off-color jokes.

All of these attitudes require that you truly know who you are—

that you do the deep work of self-awareness. As I have been hammering home in this book, you must stare down fear to disengage from negative, disempowering patterns that drive biased, reactionary behavior. Your team won't respond with trust and respect if you carry that baggage into the team room. Negative conditioning destroys resiliency. Think carefully about whether you are the chief drama maker on the team. Do you engage in negative gossip? Are you the one with the issues that nobody can understand, or the person who withdraws under the weight of never-ending burdens? Is it true that nobody can appreciate your brand of suffering? Or maybe your pattern is that the team can't live without you, so they had better treat you better. This type of fear wolf thinking holds teams back.

When you are negative, you may fall down that seventh time and not find any teammates to help you get back up again.

Self-awareness training develops humility because it puts a check on your self-importance. Training in breath and mindfulness techniques enables you to recognize that everyone is valuable and connected at some level. You become less of a drama maker, less attached to your stories. This opens up new possibilities for you—such as genuinely caring for your teammates. As *you* become less self-obsessed and important, the *team* becomes more important.

Self-awareness practices lead you to the realization that you are not your story. You will get over the fear of falling down, of not overcoming the obstacles or not being perfect or the most competent. You stop experiencing failure as personal. Failure might be happening to you, but you are not the failure, and you should not experience any shame, guilt, or blame from it. Things that happen to you and the things you do, even your great accomplishments, will stop defining you. Detach from the outcomes and embrace the growth instead. The next crisis will be your teacher—another opportunity to seek wisdom and resiliency. Use it to find humor and move beyond the drama.

PAUSE, BREATHE, THINK, ACT

When people aren't adaptable, they are the opposite of resilient—they are fragile. A challenge occurs, and they have a knee-jerk reaction to it. Teams have conditioned reactions in the same way individuals do. Those reactions lead them to reject the potential opportunity that has opened up with the obstacle. When they reject that new reality, it causes them to retreat. And they become more fragile as a result. Whole teams can collapse over collective regret, leading them into a form of paralysis where they stop trying. This fragile behavior becomes a self-reinforcing negative loop.

The answer to fragility is to develop a resiliency response. As the obstacle shows up, immediately implement the following four steps:

- **PAUSE: Stop what you are doing and thinking for a moment. This pause, when it becomes a habit, will stop the** brainstem's fear-based reaction and will allow the frontal cortex to engage. That is where all our moral reasoning, experiences, and training are stored. You want to pause and take a few deep breaths to oxygenate that area of your brain so that your reactionary mind doesn't take choices away.

- **BREATHE:** Breathe deeply to get your body and emotions under control.

- **THINK:** Observe what's happening—what and who is impacted, and what it means for your current plans. Orient to the new reality and define a new course of action given what you have learned.

- **ACT:** Decide what the smallest, most impactful next action can be—and take that action. Measure the results of the action and repeat this entire process.

Doubt is eliminated with PBTA—one obstacle at a time.

Keeping the actions small and measurable allows the team to regroup. The feedback will help them to move forward with confidence, slowly regaining momentum. Your team has demonstrated resiliency like that reed that was blown over. When it resurfaces from the mud, it is stronger, just as a bone knits stronger after a break.

Pause. Breathe. Think. Act. That's your drill.

PERSISTENCE

Persistence is how you develop the endurance to deal with the new normal of constant volatility and change over long periods of time. You never lose focus or motivation, and you never quit. You don't want to be like the SEAL trainee who has made it far into the process, displaying all the right physical skills, smarts, and mental toughness to be one of the elite, but who loses control in a single emotional moment and quits.

Persistence demands emotional control.

Emotions have the power to destroy your dreams or bring you to the loftiest heights. They will elevate you into your highest and best self or pull you down into despair and depression. If you are not emotionally aware and in control (and many are not), then there is no time like the present to start training self-awareness.

Authenticity is thwarted if you react poorly when experiencing a negative emotional state. I took a credibility hit when I lost my cool before the board of directors of CBC. Perhaps you, too, have had moments like this that you regret. Emotions are important, the spice of life. We don't want to suppress or deny them, but under certain circumstances we do want to control them. We can change their nature to be positive and can use them to inspire our teams. There is a time to express and a time to control.

Rather than learning emotional expression and control, many resort to digital distraction, smoking, alcohol, and exercise to deal with negative emotions. These are forms of repression or denial, which will block your capacity for authentic leadership—and also your ability to be a good teammate. Developing great emotional awareness and control means you can interdict and transmute negative emotions.

Uncontrolled anger, anxiety, jealousy, or feelings of inadequacy will make you look and feel incompetent. These are destructive to your self-confidence and the team's belief in you. They have no place on an elite team. The elite team will hold individuals accountable for developing this depth of emotional awareness and control. This is not just about dealing with the raw, in-your-face emotions, but the shadow fear wolf emotions that we have been touching on. Those repressed, suppressed, or projected emotional energies drive negative, conditioned reactions. Sometimes these can be even more toxic than the raw expression of emotions such as outbursts of anger. Negative conditioning doesn't make someone a bad person—I claimed earlier that we all have some form of it. What makes us more authentic and resilient is becoming aware of this negative conditioning and working to dispel it.

I have discussed how valuable therapy is for leaders. Combine it with mindfulness and you have a powerful combination of practices to develop emotional awareness and skillful control. Mindfulness practice is most often taught as a solitary practice, but it can also be done with your team. Many organizations are bringing this valuable skill into the workplace, and I recommend you do so as well.

How to Use Mindfulness with Your Team

Dedicate a period of time with your team for this drill, five minutes at a minimum. Have them just sit silently with eyes closed, paying attention to their breath. Instruct them to simply watch or notice their thoughts and emotions as these come up, not trying to concentrate on anything. The idea is to simply observe thoughts and emotions, labeling them if necessary, then letting them pass on by like a cloud in the sky. You can share challenges and insights afterward. The point here it to get the team comfortable doing these practices together and to bring the negative patterns into awareness.

Not only does this practice have well-documented stress management and health benefits, but over time you will begin to notice your main negative patterns as they come up from your subconscious into your conscious awareness. These patterns can then be brought to a therapist or coach to work on. If you objectify them and work on understanding them, their negative impact will lessen or disappear altogether. The old energy then transforms into new, positive energy. I have found the therapeutic tool of EMDR and also the Hoffman Process tools to be particularly beneficial in dealing with my own subconscious emotional patterns—most adopted from childhood.

In our Unbeatable Mind coaching program, emotional develop-ment is part of the client's integrated vertical development. I no-ticed early on that lack of emotional awareness and control is what held most of those leaders locked in subpar performance. In the daylong sessions, we work together with box breathing, somatic movement, mindfulness and imagery. In the imagery, the focus is on imagining a new future self, as well as reimagining past regrets to stare down the fear wolf. The clients speak with their boat crews about their patterns and possible alternative ways of being. Within months of joining, they start to develop a much greater awareness of their emotional world.

But the work doesn't stop there. Negative patterns run deep, and just talking about them isn't enough. So we put the clients in challenging situations to induce stress, as described in the commit-ment to growth chapter. This exposes negative emotional patterns under pressure in a controlled environment. The insights are de-briefed with the entire team, which helps them see the triggers, express the emotions, and get immediate feedback about how the breakdown occurred and why it led to diminished authenticity and trust. Alternative emotional responses are offered.

Doing this emotional work in a controlled training environment helps leaders develop greater awareness and control when obstacles arise in their daily lives. They will also take the most damaging fear wolf patterns exposed in training back to their coach, as well as the meditation bench, to work on.

When a team takes this emotional work seriously, they create a resiliency trampoline effect, whereby the whole team helps each individual bounce back from an emotional fail with genuine support. They are all in this together, and it doesn't serve anyone to be the one who drags the team down or who gossips about the breakdown in the office kitchen. They all know that at some point they will be in the cross hairs; it just depends on what the trigger is and when it is pulled. Emotions stop being issues that isolate individuals or ticking time bombs. Instead they become the focal point for team growth and resiliency. Over time, the team will develop the ability to detect when any individual brings in a negative emotion. They will feel it instantly, and rather than ignore, dance around, and resent it, as in the past. With practice they will address it with skillful, nonviolent communication.

Be persistent with this training, and you will never again let emotions get in the way of mission success.

WHAT'S YOUR WHY?

Endurance and persistence are related principles—one tends to reinforce the other. Whereas persistence is about staying the course through the inevitable emotional ups and downs, endurance has to do with raw mental tenacity, resolve—staying in the fight over the long term. This is the gritty, no-quit spirit. We just keep going at it in spite of the emotional issues. It's one thing to run a few miles three times a week. It's another thing entirely to run a hundred miles all at once. That endurance requires David Goggins-style mental tenacity.

I know plenty of leaders who have great persistence, but who are also wrecking balls with their team on their "long runs." Having the tenacity to remain positive and optimistic with your team—to not let shadow emotions interrupt your team's endurance run—is the real skill.

The number one way to develop endurance is to have a strong why around your missions, and always connect to that why when you embark on the endurance phase of the op.

Your why as a leader is quite personal. But it should align with the team's why—something we'll discuss more in the alignment chapter—so that they're mutually supportive. Then there are two strong whys to back you up when the going gets tough: your personal why for being on the team aligned with the mission of the team, and the team's why—the importance of and rationale for their actions.

Both of those work together and need to be invoked often to fuel endurance and persistence. If you want to stay in the fight, you have to remember why you're in the fight to begin with. Then that rationale has to remain front and center in your mind through a daily check-in.

Be aware that you can have the endurance to stay in the fight but be fighting the wrong battle. It is not uncommon for complacency to cause you to lose sight of the real mission, especially as you evolve. The why that drives you today will not be the same why that drives you in two to three years' time. And what was your why two years ago? Is it still powerful enough for your long endurance spells? When it changes, you will need to redefine your mission as well. What is your new why? What is it asking of you now? Does what you're driving toward currently still accord with the FITS Model? If you have clarity around the why, then the what and how are adaptable. Resilient leaders and teams keep all of that front and center.

WHAT'S WORKING AND WHAT ISN'T

Finally, the last principle of persistence is maintaining a radical focus on what's working and what's not. You develop work-arounds for what's not working, or come up with newer and better ways to do things.

You do this with a long-term perspective. This is why persistence and adaptability are related. If you keep doing the same things expecting the same results in changing circumstances, you're going to be disappointed, because the circumstances and the inputs are moving targets.

You need to be measuring, testing, and thinking about what's not working and how to do those things differently. You also want to look at doing newer, altogether different things to get to better results—that's the new definition of sanity. This requires that you put in place a process for looking at what's working and what's not and coming up with better solutions all of the time. We will see how the elite unit DEVGRU does in the chapter on alignment. This makes you an evolutionary team that allows you to persist for the duration of your professional "endurance events." Along the way, you and your team need to become learning machines.

LEARN TO LEARN FAST

The last of the three major principles tied to resiliency is to become a learning beast.

You can't know everything, and you can't learn everything. You have to choose wisely what you need to know. Learning has a significant element of choice to it. One of the key practices for learning fast is one we've mentioned before: saying no in service to the larger yes, choosing what *not* to learn so that you can focus radically on what you *should* know and learn. Develop the courage to say no to the wrong skills and knowledge in order to simplify your life. That way you will have less clutter and more time to learn the right things.

We move so fast today. Our minds are processing at breakneck speed, and we have conditioned ourselves to say yes or give tacit approval to just about anything that enters our inbox. We're overwhelmed and bogged down with too many things to learn, too many things that we think we have to know. We have to choose wisely and narrow our focus.

Once you decide what knowledge is useful, you're going to compare it to what you already know and identify any gaps. You then work to close that gap by learning what you don't know in the narrow area you've chosen to study. You've decided what to exclude so you can choose what to focus on.

Close the door on many things to focus on the most important few.

When you have narrowed your focus and are ready to learn a new skill, then analyze the sources of the new knowledge closely. Decide whether the source is trustworthy before you let it in. A good book may be enough to learn a new idea, but you will need an experienced teacher to develop a complex skill. Listening to a teacher put the information into words so you can contemplate it and ask questions to clarify context and content is the first step. Then you will go out and experience it in practice and get feedback. Rinse and repeat. For the most complex skills, such as learning musical instruments or mastering a martial art like aikido, I count out most teachers who haven't put in five to ten thousand hours of personal practice and teaching. That's a high bar—up to ten years to master the knowledge, and teaching it, before I select them as a teacher.

What will your standard be?

Due to the relative ease of starting a web-based business as an expert, including hosting a podcast and self-publishing a book, many unqualified (by my standards) people are putting themselves out there as teachers while lacking the depth of knowledge and wisdom you deserve. Ask if the teacher who will claim your valuable time and attention is credible and worthy of that time and mindshare. Good teachers don't put themselves at the center of attention. The age of the guru is past. Your deepest insights will come not from the expert, but from you as the new knowledge is embodied and tested with your teams.

Because of my long history with different martial arts, I often am asked: "What's a good martial art to get into?" I tell the seeker that it depends on what his or her goals are and who the best teacher is for him or her. The specific martial method will be clear after that research. Folks can waste a great deal of time by not asking the right questions and by working with incomplete or flawed knowledge.

Learning a martial art—indeed, learning anything new—without being clear about your why and choosing a teacher who fits can be costly. When I decided to get back into a student-teacher relationship in the martial arts, I thought carefully what my why was in terms of what training would serve me best at this point in my life. After doing some hands-on research, I settled on aikido for its focus on the peaceful resolution of conflict and working with energy. But I didn't just walk into the closest dojo to start training. I reached out to some senior aikido black belts · I knew, who told me about a teacher in my town who is highly skilled and works with a small group of students. I did a trial run for three months to test my why and to assess this teacher's character, skills, and ability to teach. I got the feedback I needed and committed myself to a long-term training plan. That process saved me a lot of time bouncing around trying out different arts and teachers.

CERTAINTY IS INCREMENTAL

It is easier to remain resilient when you are certain of the future and expected outcomes. But this level of certainty is hard to come by in a VUCA world. I don't think we can be 100 percent certain of anything external to us anymore (and certainty in the past was an illusion anyhow). Even our internal world is fraught with the biases and reactionary patterns discussed in this book. It's a wonder we can navigate life skillfully at all!

More certainty is available as we do self-awareness training to discover our authenticity and what we stand for. That is why these practices are my go-to for leadership development. Daily practice leads to incremental improvements in self-awareness, which will guide you to better decisions and actions. To achieve greater certainty in everything else outside you, incrementally master the basics of the skills you need for success. The basics once again become the foundation upon which you build your fortress of knowledge. Without that foundation, your learning is on shaky ground, teetering into opinion. Keep coming back to those basics as you seek to deepen your knowledge.

The most important aspects of learning to defend oneself are not the weapons—the kicking, punching, and grappling. They are the principles—adopting the right stance, positioning the body and balancing, then breathing and moving with the right mental attitude. Incrementally master the basics in those areas and I can teach you to defend yourself with the other tools in a weekend. It's easy to get seduced by the secret techniques and fancy takedowns while ignoring the basics. If you are confronted with an actual fight, those techniques will elude you because you are off-balance mentally and physically.

Once you gain a level of conscious competence, start to mentor others in the skill. This will lead to the embodiment of the knowledge, where it emanates from your being, not from your head. I call that unconscious competence.

This level of mastery leads to great self-confidence. You learn how to learn faster, so you can also develop certainty in other areas more quickly—and this further accelerates your learning. With aikido, I started as a white belt again, even though I have several black belts from other traditions. While it's humbling after having achieved much in other disciplines, I'm enjoying the process of emptying my cup again. I am moving along quickly because I am mastering the basics and have learned how to learn fast.

CHALLENGE THE UNKNOWN

Learning transforms fear into anticipation.

Staying in your comfort zone will lead to more fear. That is because the world will change around you while you stay still. Suddenly, what you thought you knew, what made you feel safe, is no longer relevant. Instead of diminishing fear by moving closer to the unknown, you have allowed the unknown to move farther from you through your inaction.

It is not enough to master learning and skills that you already possess or are passionate about. You will want to ask what it is that scares you or that you have a bias against, and go after that learning as well. Explore the unknowns—the edges of your comfort zone—to find out what you fear and to uncover blind spots. Commit to add those things to your learning plan. Constantly challenge yourself to learn things that make you uncomfortable.

Ignorance is not bliss—ignoring knowledge that scares you will hinder your growth. Use things that you fear to stimulate growth.

FAITH

Accept what's unknowable.

Some things are simply unknowable. You can't think your way through every problem. This is where faith comes in, and I don't mean this in a religious sense. What I mean is that you can have faith in the vast potential of you and your team to solve these types of challenges together.

When all the individuals of your team are committing to the principles in this book, magic happens. The collective intuition of the team produces surprising results. You can't truly know how or why the team came up with a certain solution—it's just there. That's intuition. Intuition is not well understood, and I think its workings are largely unknowable with today's research tools. That shouldn't prevent you from trusting it. Faith is trusting your intuition and using it to check your thinking and guide your actions without needing to know how it works.

Faith and intuition are more than beliefs—they are also a practice. Teams who have faith in their ability to solve problems, problems that don't yield to the normal analytical and decision models of the past, tend to reinforce their faith through the very application of that faith itself. Tapping into your creative genius requires that we go beyond our rationally trained brain and tune into the wisdom and intuitive intelligence of our hearts and bellies.

Two tools that I use with teams that require some faith are breath work and visualization. For example, as I mentioned earlier, my team box-breathes in silence before every important meeting. Not only does this calm everyone down and clear our minds, it gets us into a creativity-inducing state and synchronizes us to allow for new information to flow in. We are able to tap into more spontaneous knowledge. We also create that mental training space we call the mind gym. There we visualize a mental sanctuary where we can go to seek guidance from our heart's intuitive intelligence, and if we believe in a broader universal intelligence, from that source as well. It is surprising how valuable this practice is for coming up with spontaneous, creative solutions.

Another useful tool is insight meditation practice, which allows you to tap into what the Tibetan meditation experts call your *non-ordinary mind*. The ordinary mind is that part of your mind engaged in thinking and problem solving. Mindfulness meditation, as described earlier, has you watching your thoughts and emotions and disengaging from the story they represent. This liberating type of meditation reduces stress and is useful for developing metacognition of your patterns, but it is all done from the construct of the ordinary rational mind. The insight meditation skill is to learn to connect to your non-ordinary mind, where direct perception of knowledge occurs absent of structured thought. This aspect of mind is called different things—superconsciousness and witnessing, amongst others. This skill allows you to perceive information beyond thought, and at the speed of aware intention, which is much faster than thought. This takes a lot of practice, but will become an important skill for leaders in the future,

These are just some of the ways in which you as a leader can develop extraordinary abilities, with some faith that your mind has the capacity for different types of thinking beyond the rational thinking the West has mastered so well. These skills are yours to develop. If you hold a religious belief about what it means to have the power to be cognizant of unknowable things, or to heal others, or to connect to a spiritual guide, then great! That only adds fuel to the developmental fire. It's about context. Those of a religious faith contextualize these unique abilities as coming from God. I believe that these are attributes that we all have and that they can be developed.

RESILIENCY IN PRACTICE

The pace of change and the abundance of complex systems requires leaders and organizations to adapt to survive, often quickly. The complexity of big businesses these days is hard to imagine for those who don't work in them. In 2018 I was privileged to be invited to work with Shell's Gulf of Mexico deep water operations group and was impressed by the level of thought that they had put into training resiliency. The feats of engineering on and in the depths beneath an oil rig are rivaled only by those at SpaceX. I was inspired by the group's ability to solve massively complex problems through persistence, adaptability, and constant learning.

If Shell didn't provide energy safely, they wouldn't be Shell. Resiliency is not just trained once in a while—it is basic to what they do every day. According to Christian Overton, who invited me to present at their safety leadership conference, their mantra is "no harm, and no leaks." Drilling for liquid energy under very high pressures and in very deep waters requires an intense multidisciplinary focus on adapting to risk through assessment and mitigation. The Shell team asks the following questions daily to adapt to changing risk:

- **What could happen—what else, what else, what else? What are we missing?**

- **How could it happen?**

- **How could we prevent it from happening?**

- **How can we minimize harm to people, the environment, and our assets if it happens?**

- **How can we set up our systems to support safe work?**

- **How can we set up our systems to support safe failure?**

- **How can we help the worker increase situational awareness?**

Christian and her team frequently talk about "work as imagined versus work as done," a Human Performance concept brought to the forefront in high-risk industries by Sidney Dekker. No matter how much time you spend analyzing and planning what you need to do, something can and will go wrong, or at a minimum, it may not work the way you expected.

So it is critical to:

- ■ Plan as best you can with as much detail and intel as possible.

- ■ Create systems with redundancies for when something goes wrong.

- ■ Keep lines of communication wide open, and . . .

- ■ Increase situational awareness.

Adaptability and constant learning help combat complacency, which is just as deadly in the oil and gas business as it is in the military. Shell constantly pushes for continuous improvement and asks individuals to see themselves as one of the key risk factors. In other words, they ask themselves what they are missing due to their own biases, and what is it they don't know. They remain alert to the fact that what they don't know can kill them.

Normalization of risk is the enemy of resilience.

Great disasters in history often occur because what is normal changes subtly over time, making people feel like things are fine when they are not. The collapse of Enron or Lehman Brothers occurred because of this normalization of risk. Major financial crises happen for the same reason at a bigger, systemic level. Most of the time people aren't purposely pushing the bounds of ethics. They are simply unconsciously accepting greater risks over time because nothing bad has happened. They remain in their comfort zone—a dangerous bias. Leaders at Shell openly challenge their biases to get out of the comfort zones.

Christian and I discussed how hubris is one of the biggest barriers to learning and one of the greatest—but least talked about—risks in business. Confidence and ego are two different things. Shell encourages their leaders to be self-reflective, seek feedback, and to be open to different views. She says, "If you don't have a sufficient amount of humility, this doesn't usually work out very well. If you do manage to stay successful with too much ego, people will still not trust you. They may respect the person's position, but they won't respect the person, which will suck the team's true potential out the window." It is easy to fall for the notion that you have to expect some big egos when you are working with high performers. That is a stale idea and certainly not true in high-risk industries, or for that matter, in any situation. Egotistical leaders are dangerous and should not be invited to the party.

It's best to just accept that you are biased, try to learn what your most dangerous biases are, and then engage with practices and people that will challenge you to improve.

At Shell, different divisions share information and train together. When one unit changes or adds a process, it can affect the rest of the units in the system at some level. If the other units don't know about it, they could take an action that stresses the system. Christian and her team are familiar with the work of General Stanley McChrystal and hold frequent multidisciplinary team calls to synchronize vision and process. (We will look at McChrystal's ideas in the alignment chapter.) Christian pulls in people from various other disciplines for a quarterly face-to-face meeting to augment their biweekly calls. The teams tackle the tensions that arise as a normal consequence of working across disciplines to deliver safe operations. This allows the teams to connect to the higher purpose of safety—and drop their defenses.

Shell knows that recovering from a crisis can be hard for even the most mature teams. Leaders need to grieve and not pretend that they are above the laws of human nature. They must also set the conditions for recovery for the team. These are not skills taught in business or charm school. Leaders have to dig deep and be authentic to do this with grace. You have to accept the loss, take care of the team, discover the deeper lessons, and then do your best to make sure it never happens again, like McRaven did. All the while you need to allow all the members of your group to go through their own grieving process. Leading and teaming in organizations are real life. Shit happens. Teams that deal with the shit authentically are more resilient.

PERSISTENCE PAYS OFF

I went to New York after college to start a combined work-study program with NYU business school in 1985. I also started training in Zen and the martial arts and began to work toward my CPA in 1985. Lots of growth was happening then.

But I hadn't gone to the small liberal arts school of Colgate University to become an accountant—I was initially a premed student. Freshman year I took physics, calculus, English, and biology. I particularly loved the physics course, which was required for premed. With that course I learned a valuable lesson about persistence.

The class had only a midterm and a final, and I *bombed* on the midterm, or so I thought. I reacted negatively because, as a student in a ridiculously small public high school, I had never failed anything academically before. This triggered my fear wolf pattern of not feeling worthy or smart, though I wasn't aware of it cognitively. I rejected the notion that I might actually have the right stuff to be a doctor and retreated into the fear. I met with the freshmen counselor, who told me I should drop the class, but to talk to the professor first. So I did and he, too, told me to drop the class.

So I dropped the class.

I had never heard of grading on a curve. In my little high school, I always got straight As with little effort. I never thought about being the F student because, well, I was supposed to be the perfect one, you see? Perfect people don't fail. Later that freshman year at Colgate, I was comparing notes with a new fraternity brother who was a premed student in that same physics class. I was stunned to find that I had perhaps the highest grade on that midterm, *after the curve*. Crap. Quitting that class provided me with important lessons. It gave me self-awareness about trusting my intelligence. It also had another silver lining.

It changed the trajectory of my life.

At first I regretted dropping that class and was planning to retake it to continue my journey to be a doctor. But the incident caused me to slow down and contemplate my future more closely, which was new for me. At the time I was learning visualization from my swim coach and began to use it to visualize myself as a doctor. The problem was, I couldn't see myself in that future very well. What I could see, I didn't like. By doing this new visualization practice, I realized that I wasn't meant to be a doctor after all—it was my mother's dream, not mine. Had I gone that route, I never would have been a Navy SEAL leader, and I would have had a midlife crisis when I finally figured it out. Still, at that time I would rather have made that decision to walk away from medicine from a position of strength and insight, rather than quitting and regretting it. That gave me cause to study my reactions.

My fallback academic path was economics, which would prepare me for a corporate job. You read that that, too, turned out to be off target. I was convinced that economics would set me up to roll in piles of money and would prepare me to lead the family business. I plowed ahead and ended up with a very nice position in a Big Eight firm, along with the elite business school pass. That brings me back to where I started this section—in New York as an auditor while going to NYU business school at night.

It didn't take long for the universe to intercede to set me straight again, as it has a tendency to do. During my second year at Coopers & Lybrand, the CPA exam, the passing of which was required for my job, slapped me in the face. The test is broken up into four parts—theory, law, and two parts for accounting practice. If you don't pass all four, you don't pass the test. In my first attempt, I got qualifying scores on three of the parts. Back to work I went, but it wasn't as if all I had to do in life was study for that challenging exam. I was working full time, taking MBA classes at night, and squeezing my martial arts classes in the cracks. I was up studying until midnight, then would wake up at six A.M. to run the streets before work. Rinse and repeat.

Fortunately I was paying close attention to the principles I was learning in my martial arts training. In martial arts, when you get knocked down, you get up right away, ready to fight. You stay the course to fight for that black belt over the months and years, no matter how much emotional turmoil you experience. These were the life skills of resiliency that I realized I could apply to my professional life. It may sound silly now, but it was a big insight for me at that age. I had just failed the CPA exam and had remembered that the last time I failed at something, I quit. I told myself there was no way I would do that again, ever. I am glad I learned this principle at twenty-two—I have clients who are still trying to figure it out at fifty. Quitting is an emotional reaction to a fear of the obstacles themselves—where failing, losing, and not being perfect are all potential outcomes.

And I had that fear. But I committed then to overcome it. I retook the CPA exam—and failed again!

Fall down two times, get up three. I was really frustrated, but had faith in my mentor Nakamura's teachings, so six months later I took the test a third time. Finally I passed the whole thing—by one point! I didn't quit, and I knew that I would never quit anything again due to an emotional reaction.

Here is the kicker—I realized after that experience that I also had zero interest in being a CPA. It took three shots at the test and two years of hard work for me to recognize that I simply was not interested. I did, however, appreciate that experience as a means to cultivate resiliency, because I now knew that I wouldn't quit anything worthy that I committed to. That experience would benefit me in the future.

And soon it did. It helped in my persistence to get into SEAL training after the recruiters told me I had as much chance as a snowball in hell. Then it helped when I launched the Coronado Brewing Company, even if the outcome wasn't satisfying. And if I had "just" been a SEAL, especially in 1996, the investors wouldn't have trusted me to know anything about business. My four years with a global accounting firm and an MBA from a top business school brought me a ton of credibility.

My persistence in the martial arts also paid off. Had I quit that—and there were times I darn well was going to—I would have had a different story to tell. That's because earning my black belt in Seido Karate came paired with serious Zen meditation. Those four years gave me entirely new mental skills, which were instrumental in guiding me to become a better leader and a more aware person, and in enabling me to connect more deeply with others. That gave me the resiliency to be one of only nineteen graduates out of the original hundred and eighty-five in my SEAL training class. And I have already described how resiliency paid off for my business career after the military, and it continues today.

The lesson: You never know where or when your persistence will pay off. Fail forward fast and never quit. It seems too easy in retrospect.

Bottom line: Resiliency grows the more you practice adaptability, persistence, and learning. A passion for learning led me to become a learning machine. Persistence with Zen meditation led me to stop looking for approval externally, but instead to look inside and trust my decisions and myself. Adaptability in business has led me to a business that is both profitable and rewarding and helps a lot of people. And connecting to my heart has led me to deeper resiliency and compassion in my relationships with my family and teams. So yeah, basically the principles of resiliency were crucial for me to become who I am today. They work, if you work them.

Next up is the seventh principle, where battle communications, maximum sharing, and radical focus bring all the commitments, and your team, into alignment.

SDTW Exercise 7:
ADAPTABILITY, PERSISTENCE, AND LEARNING

These exercises are meant to be done with your team. They will be your daily resiliency practices.

■ **EMOTIONAL CONTROL:** Implement the Pause, Breathe, Think, Act process introduced in this chapter to interdict reactionary behavior and replace it with a positive response. This will cultivate optimism and remove fear of not knowing or of falling down.

■ **TEAM FOCUS:** In your team meetings, openly state to each teammate that you have their back. When you get more comfortable with this work, you can do this with a hand to your teammate's heart, and his or hers to yours. This is an amazing way to connect at a heart level with your teammates, so they can feel that you have their back.

■ **TEAM MANTRA:** Come up with a team mantra that will help the team feed its courage wolf and remain resilient through the challenges. My team uses: "We've got this, easy day, hooyah!"

■ **ACCELERATED LEARNING:** Implement a team mindfulness practice. After the sessions, reflect upon and/or dialogue about: personal and team why; personal and team biases; and personal and team skill and knowledge gaps.

LEADERSHIP COMMITMENT
#7

COMMIT TO
ALIGNMENT

STARE DOWN THE FEAR OF SHARING

Mike Magaraci—Mags to his friends—is a retired force master chief—the most senior enlisted SEAL in the active duty SEAL community. He now serves as director of mentorship at BUD/S, where he provides leadership, mental toughness, and character mentoring. Mags is one of the more open-minded leaders who has been instrumental in bringing nuanced mental development skills into the SEAL training program. These new skills are making a difference in developing a more resilient and aware force. But in an earlier role, Mags experienced first hand what it takes to build an elite teams of teams.

Mags was the command master chief at the counterterrorism unit Naval Special Warfare Development Group, or DEVGRU, for short. As the senior enlisted SEAL, he had a large number of talented senior leaders reporting to him—the most experienced SEALs in the entire force. Leading elite leaders can be daunting, more like taming lions than herding cats. And with an operation so disparate and full of hard-core experienced operators, the command master chief has one of the most challenging jobs. The relentless pace of combat operations—unprecedented in modern history, with the SEALs in the fight for over eighteen years without a break—greatly exacerbated that leadership challenge.

Mags focused much of his energy on preserving and refining the culture of the command. He worked this out in concert with the other master chiefs, who had the day-to-day work of leading the "shooters." In addition, he was tasked with keeping the team on the cutting edge of evolving tactics, techniques, and procedures. In that capacity he would ensure that any new tech and standard operating procedures being developed by the units were shared throughout the command and the force. This helped the global Naval Special Warfare organization to be as mission-ready as possible.

Every one of the leaders in the organization was super talented and thought that his or her way was the right way—no different from any other high-performing team. These types will get the job done alone to avoid drama and perceived incompetency. They will put their heads down and go, go, go—which also means they focus exclusively on their small part of the overall mission. Mags saw an urgent and important need to get this ruggedly individualistic team of leaders into greater alignment. How he went about it did not make him popular. In fact, there was a great deal of bitching and moaning. However, in the long run he also knew that *a bitchin' frogman will become a happy frogman.*

Alignment requires time dedicated to shifting teammate focus from crucial individual missions to synchronize with the grander picture. The perception from the operators in the field, though, is that this is an administrative distraction, and a waste of time. To be fair, they really did not have the time for such initiatives, if they were not made a priority. Mags had to make it non-negotiable with the operators.

His solution was to hold a weekly videoconference dubbed an "engaged leadership reflection session." The meeting could not be missed—no matter how many bad guys his leaders were chasing. They had to have a damn good reason to not attend. The sessions were planned for ninety minutes, but the most productive ones often went for hours. The process always followed the same sequence.

First, the commander of the team provided guidance on vision, mission, and tactical focus. This was followed by an update on big-picture hot topics from across SOCOM that the commander felt it important to keep everyone informed about. Then there were four questions by Mags for the leaders:

- **What are your tactical targets and current projects?**

- **What new technology are you testing, evaluating, and employing?**

- **What standard operating procedures are you developing? What tactics, techniques, and procedures are you utilizing that are new or significantly different?**

- **What are your morale or discipline issues, and how are you handling them?**

If leaders had nothing to share, they just said, "No input." If there was something valuable to share, leaders would present what was working, what was not working, and why. This was a good opportunity to highlight successes and the things they were innovating, as well as to be authentic in exposing failures, including their own.

Mags was optimistic that leaders would be more mission effective if they synchronized frequently on these crucial issues. Over time, the meetings offered a safe space for total transparency across all the subordinate units, as well as with the head shed. This transparency was necessary to get to a deep level of understanding and trust—and subsequently the results they all demanded of themselves. They could not hide behind veils of self-importance or mission criticality, which keep many leaders out of sync with their stakeholders.

These sessions demanded thoughtful preparation. You couldn't always, show up with nothing to share or you'd get called out for wasting time. The leaders had to think through things that might otherwise be ignored, or put off until a day that never came. The preparation alone was worth its weight in gold, forcing leaders to take downtime to think about their thinking.

The issues that surfaced in the calls were tracked, so Mags could offer support offline. The leaders began to see that their problems were not theirs alone; other leaders had similar issues, and some new ones were added to their collective learning. And they didn't have to solve them alone—their peers were eager to help. The silver lining was that the top echelon leaders were able to identify troubling trends and blind spots before they became major issues.

The tone of the sessions followed that of the SEAL debrief process pioneered by Vietnam vets like Marcinko and continued by leaders like Olson, McRaven, O'Connell, the Horra, and Luttrell. The good, the bad, and the ugly could be aired without threat of retribution. Since everything was fair game and nothing was to be taken personally, the team could remain radically focused on process and cultural improvement. Because there were no expectations of any kind of repercussions, every major screw-up came to light. It was Mag's job to sift through the ugly ones and handle them before they were mischaracterized in the media or became legal problems for the SEALs. The leaders also dealt with the more routine issues in real time to try to avoid the paperwork tsunami required of the large bureaucratic Navy. This all developed even more trust with the troops closest to the enemy bullets.

Within three months of implementing this protocol, every master chief in his command commented that they didn't know how they got by *without* the sessions. The squadron master chiefs now saw it as mission critical. It made them better leaders because they learned from one another—more specifically, from one another's mistakes.

Mags told me: "Those sessions required more time and energy than most leaders are willing to invest, but they produced pure gold. Good practices became best practices through the sharing, and new insights surfaced that were missed at the local level. What one team was working on in one hot spot was suddenly, with a slight modification, the solution that was evading a team in another. And I was able to spot trends in morale or discipline that we could get a jump on."

We learned with Shell Oil that complacency is the enemy of resiliency. When you submit to the grind and don't take time to reflect with penetrating questions, then that devil in the details will eventually throw his flaming spear at you. We've all either been that leader or worked for that leader who was heads down and mission focused, but missed the forest for the trees. Then when someone or something broke, that leader would immediately react with legalistic or administrative paper protocol. The chance that the issue could have surfaced and been dealt with at the lowest possible level by the leaders in the field is lost.

If you don't look at *why* a breakdown happens—without finger-pointing or blame-throwing—then no learning can occur. The opportunity for transformation is lost. As we have seen, most challenges of this nature are the result of emotional issues arising from shadow patterns induced by stress and discomfort—which are the norm when volatility, uncertainty, complexity, and ambiguity abuse your operation. Mags's process, painful as it was, helped to prevent the worst consequences of human nature when those humans are under severe stress. It brought everyone together in a shared experience of one team, one fight. The weekly synchronization allowed for action to address the underlying causes of stress before they became systemic breakdowns. Alignment turned out to be the critical factor that would deepen the culture of trust, respect, growth, excellence, and resiliency that already existed at DEVGRU.

While Mags was implementing his process for alignment, U.S. Army General Stanley McChrystal was running the International Security Assistance Force, or ISAF, in Afghanistan. McChrystal had to coordinate the activities of many individuals across various commands. There were multiple departments of disparate governmental and nongovernmental organizations, or NGOs, from the United States and other foreign countries within the coalition. He had units within the U.S. military special operations and conventional combatant commands, the CIA, the DIA, and the State Department, and they all had their own unique cultures and communication styles.

It's a nightmare to even consider how McChrystal could get all these warfighters, bureaucrats, politicians, logisticians, and private military contractors in sync with what mattered most. When each unit went to Afghanistan to carry out their part of the complex mission, they all tried to do things the way they always had in the past—and, no surprise, remained stovepiped and ineffective.

The enemy was much more fluid and far more unpredictable than expected. They were stomping the ISAF in the VUCA environment that they had created. It left McChrystal and his forces in complete reactionary mode—days, if not weeks, behind the enemy.

It dawned on McChrystal that he needed to take his disparate group and turn them into one team—a *team of teams*. One team, one mission, comprised of these separate teams with their own subcultures—but all with a shared consciousness. The result is what he called *empowered execution*. This was exactly the same challenge that Mags had, but at a much bigger scale, and with individuals from disparate cultures rather than a homogeneous one. It appeared to be a much harder problem to solve, but the principles were the same, and the solution was surprisingly similar. According to Mags, who had worked for the general, McChrystal told his troops that "It takes a network to defeat a network."

They set up a digital portal network to connect all the disparate forces so they could benefit from the network effect. And they had to be faster than the enemy at disseminating and understanding information. The network was the main tool for disseminating the commander's guidance down to the lowest-ranking shooter in an assault squadron. It flattened the organization, so everyone was operating off the same guidance. Another powerful analogy he used to gain organizational strength was the starfish concept. He thought the best organization structure was to be like a starfish. If a starfish loses a limb, it still functions fine because the central node is intact. The leg can eventually regenerate itself.

To foster information sharing and empowered execution, General McChrystal implemented a daily synchronization call for the key leaders from all the organizations under his vast command. They'd videoconference from wherever they were in the world, and go through a series of questions much like Mags's. McChrystal's main mission went beyond just listening and responding: he needed to curate a shared mindset that would supersede and link the disparate cultures of all the organizations. The shared mindset would be driven by clarity around vision and norms. So every single call McChrystal took the opportunity to discuss his vision and the behavioral norms he desired from this new team of teams.

He would look for key places in the call to insert the guidance— sometimes right at the beginning, but often when a probing question was asked. He would drop guidance in when it came to discussing discipline or boundary issues. He would talk about the ethos of the warrior in the field, particularly under pressure, and how the

U.S. and Allied forces were expected to conduct this war. Doing this let all of the parties involved know where they stood and what decisions they should make when confronted with the inevitable VUCA gray areas.

He broke down the rigidity of the chain of command. Everyone was a valuable team player first, then role and rank followed. The call would sometimes veer off on an issue that required deeper discussion between some of the parties, but not all. Those involved were entrusted to take it into a chat room to discuss the issue in real time. There they would share ideas and contacts, so they didn't interrupt the flow of the videoconference. In effect the organization was creating dotted lines to one another in a dynamically changing organization chart.

Those who have read the general's excellent book *Team of Teams* will recall the spaghetti-like chart depicting the lines of communication. It was not their "org chart," though some could mistake it for such. Leaders who normally would never talk were suddenly connected with a dotted line to each other, where they could share ideas, intel, and resources outside the normal chain of command. This created a decentralized network that tied together the disparate teams not connected in the centralized structure. While the paper trail still dominated the bureaucratic side of the organization, the decentralized fighting structure was amorphous and adaptive and shared information at much greater frequency, allowing teams to respond with alacrity to, rather than simply react to, the enemy.

The daily syncing up of everyone involved led to great clarity about the general's vision, as well as the team of team's values and boundaries, and enabled all involved to figure out what was working and what wasn't. This allowed the leaders to take what they learned immediately to their troops, to keep them focused on the targets. It also built in serious redundancy where everyone was focused on, or at least aware of, all the major issues of the other units. If a group needed support, they could cover that need quickly and effectively.

This distinct alignment around the mission, vision, and values of the broader team created a shared consciousness in which everyone could then operate more autonomously. The subordinate teams were empowered to execute at the lowest level, meaning that the soldier, SEAL, airman, marine, or civilian closest to the enemy was empowered to act. They could move at the speed of thought and rapid planning instead of at the speed of bureaucracy. That is how the general's team of teams created empowered execution. With that clarity, they could get busy taking it to the enemy.

The three primary aspects of alignment that warrant deeper attention in this chapter are enacting *battle communications,* maximizing *sharing,* and developing *radical focus.*

BATTLE COMMS

C reate a communications protocol as if you are in battle.

A VUCA environment requires battle footing. The business terrain is looking more and more like a special ops battlefield, so you have to create a communications process that is battle ready—we'll call that battle comms.

While McChrystal had daily meetings and Mags had weekly ones, you will have to determine what "battle rhythm" is appropriate for your team. At Shell, the largest of the teams discussed here, it is dependent on the department. But even Shell has quarterly company-wide sync-ups, and more frequent ones if a crisis is in play. In my company, I hold a weekly synchronization meeting with my key leaders, and then those key leaders have daily synchronization meetings with their teams. We also have a monthly operational sync-up and a quarterly strategic planning session.

If we use what we learned from Mags and McChrystal, it is effective to ask and answer:

- **What's working and what isn't?**

- **How do we fill the gaps?**

- **What are the culture and discipline issues? How best do we address them?**

Granted there is a lot of detail beneath all those questions—but sticking to the questions with relentless consistency meeting to meeting is the point. Rear Admiral H. Wyman Howard III, a former DEVGRU commander, told his team: "We can never be intoxicated by our successes, nor defeated by our failures, nor hide from our gaps."

All battles have a rhythm, and so does your business, so it's important that your teams sync up at the frequency appropriate for your battle. Elite teams acknowledge the different rhythms and make sure they work with them, instead of being thrown off-balance by them.

Use sync meetings to create your own music—instead of getting played by someone else's battle instrument.

When you take on a new mission or project, I suggest you immediately think about your strategy for battle comms. This is easy to take for granted, which can lead to big information and understanding gaps—gaps that can be avoided. When considering your battle rhythm, keep in mind that your organizational mission, your unit mission, and the types of team projects you take on will influence how information should flow. DEVGRU's mission is broad and doesn't change often. But each subordinate unit within DEVGRU also has its own mission, which is always changing, such as capture this bad guy or make sure those weapons are secure. The communications rhythm for each of these units is different. And when you take on a new product innovation or process improvement, those new targets will produce yet another layer of information flow. My point is that, given this complexity, be thoughtful about how you synchronize information flow to ensure engaged awareness among your units—at all levels.

This will lead to great alignment and then greater momentum.

BULLSHIT MEETINGS CRUSH ALIGNMENT

On the other side of the coin, we have all experienced "death by meeting." I am not suggesting above that you add meetings just to share ideas, especially if you already have solid alignment. No doubt many meetings are a complete waste of time and crush the team's can-do, will-do spirit. However, you must agree that it is impossible to work as a team without effective communications, and most teams fall short on this simple point.

When done poorly, meetings suck the life out of an otherwise perfectly fine day. Worse, they can shut down the type of open, heart-centered communication that is necessary for your team to soar. If a meeting has a clear purpose and structure, it is worth the collective weight of the participants in gold. In effective meetings, the purpose of the meeting and the agenda are clear, and only those individuals who absolutely need to be there are present. The meeting is as short as possible to get the information shared and processed and requisite decisions made. However, it is also imperative not to rush to fit into a time block, as Mags found out. Most important, include guidance around purpose, vision, mission, and norms in *every single meeting.* Any time your teams are together, in person or via technology, you have an opportunity to deepen alignment.

Most companies have functional meetings for departmental work. These are necessary. I would also consider forming specialized teams for training, who will assess and mold the team's horizontal and vertical development, as well as meetings for target selection, where the team will use the FITS Model to assess current and near-term targets to make sure they are legitimate. And I recommend adding a specific gathering just for alignment, like Mags's and McChrystal's meetings. Ensure that a *brief* and a *debrief* is conducted for every major initiative or "mission." These last two meeting types have a unique protocol and help special operators remain radically mission focused.

The Brief: The brief is the presentation of the SMEAC battle plan for how you will attack your target. SMEAC is one version of the SOF mission planning process, and stands for Situation, Mission, Execution, Administration/Logistics, and Command/ Signal. Each one of these areas is given thoughtful consideration by their responsible experts and then briefed by those same parties. The overall mission leader hosts the brief. The purpose of this meeting is to align around the mission, ensuring explicit and implicit goals and objectives are clear. Also, it is an opportunity to rehearse the op by visualizing it with the entire team, which is why SOF operators include a lot of pictures and videos in their briefs.

The Debrief: The debrief, of course, happens after the mission is complete and the target is secured. The debrief should happen for each stage of the op, if your mission is of long duration. The debrief involves asking probing questions, making observations about how things went overall, and assessing team and individual performance with an eye toward constant improvement. As mentioned before, the tone of these meetings is monumentally important. Similar to how Mags ran his meetings, no personal attacks, shaming, guilting, or any fear wolf pack attacks are allowed. Period. The meetings would lose all of their value, and the main points—the learning and alignment that comes from these powerful sessions—would be lost.

With all battle comms egos must be checked at the door with no disengagement or disruption allowed. If anyone is disruptive, it should be dealt with immediately and a boundary set in place for future sessions. Either the disruptive person gets on board with the rest of the team, or they are asked to leave.

That isn't to say you are looking at the team to rubber-stamp your vision and ideas. Nor do you want groupthink or fantastical thinking. Instead you are asking them to ask and answer the hard questions—to get beyond the biases that impact group dynamics. All views should be expressed in a thoughtful, emotionally mature manner. Everyone must be properly prepared and practice active listening and engaged questioning, rather than damaging the team's energy with judgment and righteousness. Distractions such as cell phone interruptions are not allowed, except in emergencies.

Incidentally, meeting follow-up is another important aspect of battle communications. I have been to many meetings where it was agreed that so-and-so will take on a project, and then there is radio silence afterward. VUCA gets in the way and other urgent or important things pop up. At the next meeting, it is like nothing was said previously. That is horrible accountability, which made me feel completely ineffective when I was the leader.

Good battle comm protocols can nip that problem in the bud. The team leader will send the desired outcomes and agenda in advance, and then a meeting summary with to-dos and assigned tasks afterward. That summary will include any insights and alignment guidance the leader has after digesting the meeting. The point here is to deliberately use these meetings to evolve the team through a process of continuous learning and cultural alignment.

When there is a crisis, the battle comms will take on a different level of urgency. A crisis can paralyze a team, so it helps to train for crises and develop a contingent battle plan. That will ensure that communication doesn't break down as a result of the crisis. If there is an ambush on an op, the SEALs kick into crisis action mode. First, they would immediately take control of their individual physiological and emotional responses. They do this through the deep breathing, positive internal dialogue, and emotional control tactics. Next, they will focus on getting "off the X" (target) and maintaining the integrity of the team with any triage needs. Then shift fire to any immediate threats to provide cover from the enemy. They then activate the OODA loop (observe, orient, decide, and act) to determine their next response. Finally, they will alter their plan and communication strategy to deal with the new reality, and execute. They are all set to respond positively and proactively with the new plan. After the crisis is over, they will conduct a debrief to learn and improve for future ops. That process works in any setting, not just on the actual battlefield in war.

WIN IN YOUR MIND
BEFORE THE BATTLE

Battle comms are not just about communicating with the team. It is also how you communicate with yourself! When in the fight, treat every day like a performance event. You can prepare by "winning in the mind before stepping into battle." This takes the battle comm alignment principle into your inner relationship with yourself. Then teach your team the drill to win in their mind to maintain peak performance throughout the day.

Let me use my personal battle comms as an example. My morning starts with box breathing. Then I reflect on my purpose and mission, performing a short meditation and future-self visualization. Finally I mentally walk myself through the day, outlining what I am planning to do and visualizing myself being very successful at it (the dirt dive). In addition, I will prepare for snags by trying to anticipate anything that could go wrong and coming up with a positive response to the snafu. This preparation process takes only twenty to thirty minutes and sets the optimal conditions for my performance throughout the day.

During the day, when in the fight, I dedicate time for deep work as well as the alignment stuff. I take frequent recovery breaks for spot drills, which include deep breathing, somatic movement, strength training (longer time needed for this one), active listening, meditation, time outside on a mindful walk, and the like. I will allow my intuition to guide me about what is necessary. I will also mentally prepare for important meetings or events and conduct personal after-actions as necessary.

Then after the professional day's "fight" is over, there is a time to book-end the day. That practice is to mentally go back and review what happened—what went well, what didn't. This is like a daily synchronization meeting with yourself.

I ask:

- **What are my biggest insights and lessons from the obstacles?**

- **How has the day made me better? What did I learn?**

- **Did my actions move me toward my vision and goals?**

- **Any unresolved issues or unanswered questions I need to follow up on?**

This strategy helps keep me aligned around the important and urgent aspects of my purpose and mission.

Battle comms create a powerful mindset that embodies all of the core principles in this book: courage, trust, respect, growth, excellence, and resiliency. And it gets you and your team aligned for maximum effect. We would say in the SEALs: "The way you do anything is the way you do everything."

The way you communicate with yourself and with others will determine how the team creates shared meaning and intentionality. It requires a lot of discipline to do this well. Self-management, the frequency of team communications, meeting norms, rules and intentions, the positive attitude and emotional state of the team, openness and transparency, and a nonjudgmental culture all come into play. Communicating like this is not easy, but it is definitely worth it. You don't need to have the life-and-death risk of Shell oil roughnecks, the SEALs, or the ISAF warriors to experience the enormous benefits.

MAXIMIZE SHARING

A central theme of this book is that your team is your primary mechanism for growth as a leader. Individuals who commit to grow together and work toward a common mission will achieve greatness together. So far we have seen how alignment is a consequence of relentlessly communicating vision, norms, and intent. However, that is not enough to ensure complete alignment around intent. The leader and team must also be willing to share experiences and be exposed to the same level of risk in order for all of the commitments discussed in this book to flourish.

All teammates, including the positional leaders, must be willing to maximize sharing—starting with information, experiences, and risks. As the team opens up to experiencing what everyone else is thinking *and* feeling from their various perspectives, they begin to appreciate that all have similar fears and vulnerabilities. They will see that the team's strength lies in acknowledging its imperfections so the team can then fill the gaps and protect one another from biased decision-making. With elite teams, there's no hiding, whether in your office or behind some facade. You have to be willing to share it *all*.

Mags was willing to go to the hot spots and run ops with the team. McChrystal would routinely be out in the battle space, putting himself at great risk to ensure he shared the experience of the shooters and the intel gatherers. McRaven risked his own life and reputation to share experience with his operators, as did Olson and O'Connell. These individuals understood that to do their job well they had to get out of the office and share information, their ideas, their support—and take risks with the team. This allowed the leaders to get out of their heads and into their hearts, and for the team to experience that side of them. It's also how they developed the intuitive capacity for better decision-making when VUCA showed up.

Trust is diminished when a leader doesn't share. In one of my early leadership roles at SEAL Team Three, I was supported by a senior enlisted leader. He was a great guy and regaled us all with humorous stories of his days in the jungles of Vietnam. Apparently he had been in a number of helicopter crashes and was spooked any time we trained with helos. I noticed that when the team was training for parachuting, rappelling, or fast-roping into a target, he inevitably had some urgent requirement to be somewhere else. I understood what was going on and was sympathetic, but I also knew that the team noticed. They resented that he was not sharing risks and experiences with them. Yes, he had "been there and done that" back in the day, but this is today. What are you doing for the team today?

Never rest on yesterday's accomplishments.

Finally I had to confront this individual. I told him the men were noticing that he wasn't sharing the air training risk with them, and that he was not leading from the front as a senior leader should. He confessed to me his fear of crashing again, saying that he was trying to avoid "unnecessary air tragedy." I explained what his actions looked like from the perspective of the other warriors—that their trust in him was diminishing. He never missed another air operation after that.

Had he not been willing to share that risk with the team, I would have had to ask him to leave the platoon. It was that important.

Everyone on the team must be "all in, all the time."

If you as a leader don't share experiences, you'll flat out lose the trust and respect of the team—the two commitments that are the most difficult to gain. If you are *not* willing to share the risk, then you should take the lead to depart from the team before being asked to leave. This also speaks to those you select to be on the team to begin with, because if you can't anticipate and select for this trait, then you will have to deal with issues down the road that can be disruptive and slow you down. Build a team that is willing to take off their masks, and maximize sharing.

It should be noted that when I say you must be willing to do what you ask your team to do, I don't mean to imply you do something in which you're not trained. For example, in the SEALs I would not free-fall parachute jump with my team if I wasn't qualified. Taking part in something that puts the mission at risk due to your lack of training or competence is worse than not sharing risk. There are appropriate ways to share exposure and risk, and it will differ for every individual and situation. In that situation, I would endeavor to get the requisite training and would support the team with the jump in a manner appropriate for my level of training—perhaps observing from the aircraft. Share the level of risk appropriate for your skill level, qualification, and job position. The point is not to hide behind that position or your office door when the hard stuff goes down.

Similarly, as much as you can, it is good to share the general workday experiences of other teams that you interact with. Everyone works in a team of teams now, and they will all appreciate your going to where these teams are getting their real work done. Go into the field and get a sense for what's going on with all the units. It's not enough to see the entirety of an operation on an org chart.

Elite teams get out of their silos and share in one another's experiences. For Shell, that means getting out of the office and onto the oil rigs and refineries. For the SEALs, it is at the forward operating bases where the teams are staging their nightly ops. This also requires some discretion, as nobody is served by your disrupting their operations for a dog and pony show. You want to be more than a name on an org chart, but not suck the oxygen out of the air when you arrive at the FOB. Senior military and political leaders often have that effect when they go to the front lines, even with the best intentions.

We have already discussed how important it is to share more information. Alignment requires relentlessly sharing vision, mission, and norms. Sometimes, though, we move so fast that we don't take the time to share other important information. Or, equally likely, that information is held close for power and prestige. I don't recommend you be an information hoarder. It is especially necessary to quickly share insights and lessons about what's working and what isn't; what we think might happen; and about what we learned from what *did* happen.

Is it possible to share too much? Probably. My tendency to share future product and business ideas with my team didn't work out well. They would get distracted or stressed because they took these ideas as action items, when I was just seeking feedback to test the idea. So you must share "need to know" information, but not information that doesn't impact the team now or in the near future. Save that for future planning sessions. But, consider that more information is "need to know" in VUCA than less, so don't hoard it. Free flow of information helps the team get a sense for where the battle is moving, what direction to be facing. This helps to create that shared consciousness.

As we have discussed, now is the time to share leadership, too. Top leaders don't hoard their leadership authority. Without abdicating accountability, they will share responsibility for leading so others can gain experience and build trust. Elite team leaders acknowledge that they don't have all the answers, that the team is the ultimate leader, and that they're just temporarily in charge. They actively share leadership opportunities, looking to get out of the way and allow others to lead.

These practices are how a team grows and taps into the collective brilliance of the entire group. When everyone sees themselves as always leading and always following, then the traditional hierarchical structure softens into a real team, in which the whole is greater than the sum of its parts. Both the team and the leaders empty their cup daily, asking, "Who is best to lead this charge? And how can we support him or her?" Your success is my success. This approach allows the team to solve challenges as a group instead of a single leader trying to direct the outcome.

The unique passions of each team member should also be shared. Not only will trust and authenticity be deepened, but you never know when someone's hobby will come in handy. With special ops teams, everyone is both a generalist and a specialist. The entire team trains relentlessly in the general skills—for example, shooting, moving, and communicating. However, the specialized skills draw on the passion of the individual and are trained individually. The best teams share this specialized knowledge and use it to deepen the team's capability.

A company will spend valuable resources to train general job skills, but will often deny teammates the time and money to pursue unique passion skills, which could bring valuable strength to the team. In a VUCA environment, you might be surprised by the knowledge that leads to a breakthrough. Those who have unusual skill sets can be part of brainstorming to provide perspectives beyond the generalist's purview.

Share your best self with the team to bring out the best in your teammates. When you merge your consciousness with the team like this, it changes you and the team for the better. At the same time, you don't lose yourself—you become more aware of who you are—your strengths, weaknesses, passions, and impact on others. And since your power is greatly enhanced due to the multiplicative effect of your team's helping you succeed, you feel more motivated to discover your innate strength. You find yourself with more power, more purpose, and an ability to connect deeper with all who you interact with—including your family.

In this way, the team becomes a powerful leadership unit—more powerful than a gathering of individuals working together, and far more powerful than when an individual leader hoards all the responsibility.

RADICAL FOCUS

The ability to apply radical focus to a target is another hallmark of an elite team. In the SEALs, we were trained to seek the smallest actions that would lead to the biggest results. Then we would radically focus on those actions to completion. We would repeat this process until we dominated. The ability to point many minds toward a single target, with laser precision, leads to extraordinary results. This is how McRaven's team nailed Bin Laden and countless other high-value targets when he directed SOCOM.

A good way to practice this intense focus is to have a set of focusing questions for yourself and the team to ask daily. By answering these questions on a regular basis, you will continually realign your plan on the fly. Here are mine:

- **What will move me closer to fulfilling my personal vision and mission today? My team's vision and mission?**

- What is the most important target for me to focus on today, and what action can I take now to move forward?

- Is what I'm about to do in alignment with my own and my team's ethos and what we stand for?

- How can I find greater alignment with and bring greater clarity to the team today?

- Does my plan for the day include shared experience, risk, challenge?

- How and when will I communicate with the team today?

- Could anything I'm planning—or not planning—take me out of alignment?

- What are the biggest potential distractions to be aware of?

- Is there anything else I can do to keep the team radically focused and battle-ready?

Answering these questions allows me to see how to do something a little bit differently—maybe a little bit better than I had planned. It leads to a constant 80–20 style of culling tasks and to-dos from your list while adding better actions and refining those that remain. When VUCA arrives, you are focused on the right things for the right reasons, and can quickly shift fire to address an emergent situation.

TRAINING FOR COMBAT

The Iraq War and the insurgency that followed involved a new type of fight that required SEALs to do things in a whole new way. Before this war, SEAL training was more static. We were handed a target, planned the attack, and then took that target down. Then we went home. And we didn't cooperate well with other units, either—definitely not a "team of teams" mindset.

That situation required an entirely new mindset and training method.

The SEALs shifted their training from hard targets, like attacking a land-based missile silo, to soft targets like protecting the new Iraqi leaders, rescuing kidnap victims, and hunting really bad terrorists. It required real-time intelligence and a persistent presence in the field. Though our prior training prepared us for situational VUCA that we initiated, we needed to learn how to operate in an environment of persistent threats.

In situational VUCA, you're in control for a large part of the time and have a plan for the shit storm, which will occur at a time and place of your choosing. For us, that was when we hit the target, ready for chaos until the problem was solved. After the op, things went back to normal. With this new war we found ourselves in control of nothing except our attitudes.

Maybe it's good idea to get used to being in control of nothing but your attitude as well.

The SEALs quickly realized that the old way wasn't going to work and had to think like Marcinko to break the mold again. So the teams reorganized to be more flexible. They also saw the need to operate more closely with other Navy units deployed at the same time, such as the Explosive Ordnance Disposal (EOD) technicians, the communicators, and the air squadron, so they invited these others to train with them.

I was hired by the SEALs in 2005 after I demobilized from war to help lead pre-deployment war-preparation training—the same training I had helped create and run when recalled to active duty by Captain O'Connell.

My team put the units through a rigorous scenario-driven, intelligence-infused multi-mission training event. The objective was to emulate, as best as possible, the combat environment they would face. They had daily sync meetings with all the leaders, and then the operating units would have theirs. As the overall training head, I set the battle comms and rhythm. The teams would receive an initial mission tasking; then we injected a host of intelligence "triggers" into the scenario. These triggering messages would require some action, such as meet with an informant, recon a suspected weapons cache, etc. The teams would take the action and find new intel, which would further mold their plans.

The teams were constantly adapting plans on the fly, which was jarring at first. We constantly changed the scenarios and forced them to be responsive, not reactive. They learned to develop a very rapid planning process and a blisteringly fast operational rhythm. They had to get ahead of the OODA loop of the mock enemy or the situation would blow them over. Though the war would be far more complex than we could possibly simulate, this training helped them appreciate the real battle they would face.

The teams had to stare down the fear wolf collectively to learn to control their reactionary behaviors now, so they wouldn't react negatively in combat. Remember "the more you sweat in peace, the less you bleed in war"? The operators developed great trust and respect for one another. They learned to see the others as just like them, with an intense desire to destroy the enemy. The unrelenting battle communications created unity and that collective consciousness, as well as radical focus on the mission. Each of the commitments discussed in this book were observable outcomes.

And these teams later dominated in combat.

It was a great moment for me, as an entrepreneur and a SEAL officer, to help my military team develop that important training solution. Later, in 2006, my company was hired to create and launch the nationwide SEAL Mentor program (as discussed earlier), and as I write these words, I am again honored to help my teammates with mental toughness and character training.

It seems as if my entire life—all the hardships, the challenges, the screw-ups; and my own family dynamics—had been perfectly architected to prepare me for this important work. Do you have a sense that things in your life, even the shitty things, happen for a reason? Can you see a directionality in your life? Do you feel that perhaps if you got out of your own way, you would flourish? I do . . . and have learned to listen to the inner voice of my heart as a result. It has always served me well.

We all desire to be more authentic leaders and to fulfill our mission alongside an elite team in the face of the relentless VUCA. But fear and our shadows will hold us back, even if we're unaware of those fears and shadows. Nobody is perfect; everybody brings some baggage into their leadership. The question I want you to consider now is: *What fear do you need to stare down first?*

Can you commit to stare it down and further unlock your potential? I am confident you can and suggest you start with the exercises for these seven commitments. But before you head to your training space to get started or back to your team to get busy, I have one more commitment for you to consider.

SDTW Exercise 7:
BATTLE COMMS, MAXIMIZE SHARING, RADICAL FOCUS

1. **IMPLEMENT BATTLE COMMS.** Consider the current state of your team's battle comms. Do you see alignment and shared consciousness? Are you all in sync with the rhythm of your particular battle? What can you do better in terms of how often you have meetings, how you run them, how and when you share vision and standards? Finally, do you have a process to win in your mind before entering your battles?

2. **MAXIMIZE SHARING.** Do you share risk and your authentic self with the team? What can you do better? What about transparency of information and sharing leadership? Look for ways to get out of the way and let others shine.

3. **GET RADICALLY FOCUSED.** Print out the list of focusing questions and put them where you can see them easily during the day. Periodically take a look and ask them to help you radically focus on the right tasks.

CONCLUSION
THE FINAL COMMITMENT

STARE DOWN THE FEAR OF COMMITTING TO A BIGGER MISSION

There is a kind of silence you can't hear indoors, no matter how thick your walls are, no matter how quiet your neighborhood, no matter how deep into the night you try to listen for it. The kind of silence I'm talking about is the silence of nature. If you've ever spent extended periods of time in the wilderness, you've certainly experienced it—as if the world is pausing to take a breath.

One of my favorite places to listen for this kind of silence is in the 6-million-acre Adirondack Mountains of Upstate New York. In the heat of the midafternoon, when the sun is right overhead and the shadows of the maple and oak trees have shrunk down almost to nothing, there are moments of such stillness that if you listen hard enough, you can hear the blood running through your veins.

I experienced that same silence when I deployed to Kenya for a special ops advisory mission and visited a big game reserve. I was struck by the expansiveness and beauty of our planet's open spaces, but saddened to learn how poaching and trophy hunting was destroying wildlife in Africa at an alarming rate.

A few years later I met special ops warrior turned philanthropist, Damien Mander. This meeting reinforced my positive view of humanity's ability to evolve and to defeat the dark energies of violence and exploitation. Damien knows something about silence, having spent countless hours alone in the million-acre game preserves of South Africa and Mozambique. There he has run teams whose mission is to counter poachers, who come from well-financed syndicates selling the poached elephant tusks and rhino horns for a fortune. The success of these teams and the unconventional way they are solving multiple interlocking challenges in VUCA situations solidified my belief that leaders and teams who embrace the seven commitments, and sign up for a bigger mission, can make a huge difference in the world.

STOP INVESTING IN VIOLENCE

Damien was first a clearance diver in the Royal Australian Navy. I worked with this exceptional team when I deployed to Australia in 1993, well before Damien's time in the unit. The clearance divers did salvage diving, mine countermeasures, maritime tactical operations such as vessel boarding, and underwater explosive ordnance disposal. After 9/11, Damien put in a request to join the newly formed Tactical Assault Group, which had a mission similar to DEVGRU. It was formed out of Australia's 2nd Commando Regiment. I will let him tell the story through our conversation, which was recorded for my *Unbeatable Mind* podcast.

MARK: How many Navy guys were in the Tactical Assault Group?

DAMIEN: Not many. We had a water troop, made up of a very small team. After some time with them, I became a qualified special forces sniper.

MARK: Can you tell me about your experiences transitioning from being a sniper in Iraq to coming back to the civilian world? So many get lost. How did you find meaning again?

DAMIEN: Iraq's a tough one, eh? When you're there at ground level it's hard to come up and see things from 30,000 feet. Interesting to hear of your mission with the Courage Foundation to help vets with PTS and to lower their risk of suicide. For a lot of us guys who served in Iraq, the real war doesn't start until the bullets stop, and you're trying to figure out your relevance in life.

You come from a world where you mean everything to everyone around you. And then all of a sudden, when you come home, it feels like you're by yourself. There are no work postings for "sniper" in the local newspaper when you come back home. And I suppose a reflection of why we go to war in the first place, and what that war is about, is part of that return process. It was tough. I suppose the thing that hit me hardest about Iraq was seeing what happened to the Iraqi people . . . It was just a country that was flattened, man.

While there, I made a strong effort to learn Arabic and embed myself with the culture. That served me very well. To learn their culture, you break bread with them. And when you're breaking bread, you become a part of their family and their household. I didn't meet one person there that wasn't directly affected by the war. And when I say *directly affected*—I mean, someone's kid who wasn't missing an arm from a bit of shrapnel, or a wife who hadn't been killed, or a grandmother had caught a stray bullet. And there were a handful of different wars going on over there. It's hard to know which bullets got whose name on them.

MARK: I know, war is such a tragedy. It seems to be part of the human condition, but I don't subscribe to the belief that it will always have to be that way. As more people evolve to what I call the fifth plateau world-centric perspective, the more culturally we will find war abhorrent. Interestingly, I heard an interview between Deepak Chopra and a yogi named Sadhguru, a really funny guy. A guest asked them both: "What would you guys do about the migration crisis from war-torn regions like Syria and Yemen? Would you be compassionate, or would you take the more stern approach and prevent the migration from happening?" And Deepak said, "Of course, compassion." He gave kind of the answer one would expect.

But Sadhguru just smiled and said, "You know what? I would ask that we stop investing in violence."

Right on. Why not stop investing in conflict? Those people are getting their guns and bullets from somewhere. Why *don't* we stop making the military grade guns, bullets, and nukes?

Yes, it's more complicated than that, but could world-centric leaders and teams begin to think that way? I believe so. Anyways, I went off on a little tangent. But this Navy SEAL and SAS sniper agree on that point.

So, Damien, coming back from war you felt lost and needed to find a purpose. That is what happens to a lot of guys and girls who are suffering from postwar stress experience. They lose their sense of purpose.

But you found yours, though. Tell us how.

DAMIEN: I didn't join the military to serve my country. I did it for adventure. I didn't go to Iraq to help the situation. I did it to make money. I left Iraq in 2008 and went to South Africa to decompress. I suppose when I arrived in Africa, instead of looking for a cause, I was looking for a fight. I spent eleven months there doing far too many drugs and too much alcohol, and I fucking hit rock bottom.

I was at a crossroads. I'd heard about anti-poaching about a decade before, and it was a topic of conversation there. *Hey,* I thought, *that sounds like a bit of a romantic adventure I could get myself into.*

And when I got into it, there were a couple of things I experienced that changed my life. One was seeing park rangers who left their family behind for up to eleven months of the year to be out there doing something greater than serving one's self. I'd come from a world where we were defending resources in the ground, and I had all the resources I needed.

But these guys were defending the heart and lungs of the planet. They were in a hostile area where the biggest threat wasn't so much the poachers they're trying to stop, but the animals they're trying to protect. And that really made me reflect on my life. It made me feel like shit, actually. There I was trying to have an adventure on the back of their hard work.

The second thing was the animals themselves. In combat it's a two-way street when the bullets are flying. And with these animals, it wasn't. It was such an unjust act, to kill those animals for the ivory or the sport of it. And that affected me in a way that it probably wouldn't have a decade before. Iraq had a way of breaking down my barriers and gave me a different lens to look at the world through.

Animals don't want a car, a paycheck, a bigger house. They don't have egos like us. Animals want one thing. They want to live. And we as a species continually take that away from them.

So that was enough for me to say, "Screw it." I'd done all right through real estate and I had a unique set of skills as a special operator, so I sold everything and set up the International Anti-Poaching Foundation. That was almost a decade ago. It's now registered in four countries and operating throughout southern and East Africa. The rangers we've trained and supported protect over 5 million acres of wilderness and the millions of animals of all different shapes and sizes that live there.

MARK: That is amazing work. Help us understand the world of poaching. Why is it done? What are the economics of it?

DAMIEN: There are different types of poaching. The most common is subsistence poaching, which is locals trying to put food on the table genuinely. I don't have much of an issue with them. But then there is the commercial poaching. Commercial poaching is mainly for ivory from elephants and horn coming from rhinos. Those two animals are the most aggressively targeted species. The poachers can get $35,000 U.S. a pound for rhino horn on the black markets in China and Vietnam.

And one rhino can easily have twenty or thirty pounds. These animals should be actually locked up in safes, not running around in areas the size of small countries.

When we set the organization up, it was designed to be a surgical instrument to go to the front lines and protect these animals in their natural environment. Run like a spec ops mission.

MARK: So, your concept initially was to send tactical teams out and "counter-poach" by going after the poachers. Would you actually kill them? Or would you just try to round them up and have them arrested?

DAMIEN: You try and round them up. Not only individually going after these guys—I say guys, 'cause it's mostly men doing the poaching. But we were training local forces as well.

Most of the job was making sure we had well-motivated and well-led teams in the field. The difference between success and failure in many of these operations is usually just one good commander who can pass on all the skills and, most importantly, spend time with them. We set out first to train rangers and run operations, and we grew as an organization. We learned a ton fast, and I applied a lot of what I took away from Iraq. It was constant evolution cutting away the parts that didn't work and keeping the bits that did. And pushing on, trying new things, not being afraid to make mistakes.

We made some monumental mess-ups in those early years, but we were prepared to make them and to grow from them.

MARK: What impact did that first phase of your operation have? Did you have a way to measure it?

DAMIEN: The biggest project we ran was on the border of the huge Kruger National Park in South Africa, home to a third of the world's rhino population. Most of those rhinos are in the southern quarter of Kruger National Park, Kruger shares a border with Mozambique. In 2015, you had 80 percent of poaching coming across that border from Mozambique into the heart of the biggest rhino population in the world.

Now, amazingly, there are around four hundred organizations specializing in rhino conservation in South Africa. But none were working on that piece of land that was up against the South African border with Mozambique. The piece of land that separated most of the world's rhino and most of the world's rhino poachers is the most critical piece of land on the planet for rhino conservation. So we went in there and set up a ground offensive. We involved 165 personnel and four different government departments. We built a bigger fence, brought in the guns, helos, and planes—the whole thing. It was essentially a ground level insurgency that we were fighting, and it was against the local population. We were literally at war with the local population there. But we stopped poachers coming through that area. They were international poachers going after the rhino horns, making significant amounts of money, driving brand-new cars and living in big houses.

This led to the first downturn in rhino poaching globally in a decade.

That program was a success, but it was also a big failure, because we were at war with the local community. They were all involved in supporting the poaching because they needed the money. It was literally the same thing I saw in Iraq, with locals supporting the insurgents because they were getting paid to and they needed to feed their families.

MARK: And one operation to stop one group of poachers wasn't going to change the basic underlying economic conditions that led to it to begin with. You have to address the underlying economic conditions, right? We sort of missed that in Iraq, too.

DAMIEN: Right. Not only that, but people's husbands and sons and uncles were coming home in body bags. There were over four hundred people from those communities, who were part of the poaching, killed during those operations.

G.I. JANE TO THE RESCUE

Though it drove a downturn in rhino poaching, I saw it was definitely not the answer. It made us start to think outside the box and look for something new. What we came up with will define the future of conservation, and perhaps leadership itself, as we know it.

MARK: That's the Akashinga program, right?

DAMIEN: Yeah. We were reading a *New York Times* article about the first group of female U.S. Army Rangers to go through training. And we thought that conservation is a male-dominated industry, with 100 to 1 men over women on the front lines. So I read more and more about how the empowerment of women is the single greatest force for positive change in the world today. I thought that if women don't get exposure at the ground level, they will lack the experience needed to rise up the ranks and fill management and senior positions. So instead of lamenting about not enough women leading things, we need to get them into the pipeline for leadership.

So we set out to build a female anti-poaching unit. But we couldn't find a reserve that would accept them—even a trial run. They perceived it to be a huge risk. But finally we found an abandoned trophy hunting reserve.

Now, just to give some context there. Trophy hunting is a dying industry. Trophy hunting is where people from overseas come over and shoot an elephant or a rhino for fun.

MARK: Facebook [social media activism] is helping to kill that off, right?

DAMIEN: Yeah. It is. Also, reduced wildlife populations and tougher laws and penalties around the import and export of trophies. But there was this area the size of France in Africa that is set aside for trophy hunting. And in Zimbabwe where I live, 20 percent of the landmass of that country is set aside for trophy hunting. Where trophy hunting was used as an economic model to fund anti-poaching in the past, as it dies off, the land that was set aside for trophy hunting will offer no protection from poachers. Sad irony, right?

As these areas are dying off, all the hunters that call themselves "conservationists" are moving on to the next area where there's something left to shoot. And people like us have to pick up the pieces.

We did selection for a hundred and eighty-nine men in 2012, and at the end of day one, we had only three left. Just three who were suitable to move on! I thought we would see something similar with the women but was stunned to see the results. We moved into that area in August 2017 to set up the female ranger training, starting with eighty-seven applicants. After our interview process, we had thirty-six start the selection training, which was modeled on the special operations pillars of misery: cold, wet, tired, and hungry.

At the end of seventy-two hours, only three had voluntarily dropped out. We knew then that we had something unique. I believe that the distance one places between suffering and breaking is what defines the spirit of an individual. And it's that spirit that we needed—I can train the rest. I need spirit, I need character. And these women had it in spades.

My small team of former special operations instructors put these women through hell. And they impressed us at every turn. They went operational in October of the following year

Previously, when we built an anti-poaching unit, we would recruit from around the country. Note that the local population has been pushed off the land to create the preserve to begin with, so there's already tension. And then you bring in this external ranger force not connected to the locals. They are not friends with them, not influenced by them, and not talking to them.

We decided to recruit 100 percent from the local communities. That means that the conservation was now a community investment. And 62 cents from every dollar we spend on the teams goes directly back into the local community. It doesn't go to the government or the big chief anymore, where it never trickled down the locals.

MARK: You mean that the pay that these women get goes back into their local communities because they're going to spend it there?

DAMIEN: Right! Everything needed for their ops is also purchased from the local community. And the salary of these women is hitting the community at the household level—coming from the women. There is now more money going into those communities every thirty-four days than what trophy hunting provided in a year. Conservation money is now going into the hands of women, and research tells us that women spend three times more of their salary on family and local community needs than men do. So around 90 percent of what they earn, they invest back into their local community.

Without planning this, our strategy took the conservation dollar and turned it into a community investment. And we put female empowerment at the top of the strategy. That gave the greatest bang for the buck for community development. And what was supposed to be the main thing, conservation, became the by-product.

The program also de-escalated everything. The men wanted to shoot the bad guys. But the women wanted to have a conversation, to find out what their problems were and to help fix the problems, not shoot at everything that moved. As we de-escalated, we had a less militarized approach, which is also a cheaper one.

MARK: Like Sadhguru advised—stop investing in more conflict. Start investing in the communities instead.

DAMIEN: It's completely shifted two decades of military law enforcement and conservation thinking for me.

MARK: You are still training these women how to shoot, move, and communicate, though, right? I saw the picture of one of your trainees. She looked like a Navy SEAL sniper. You're still training them to do that, but their inclination isn't to lead with the weapon first, but with an open hand.

DAMIEN: Yes. We hope for the best, but also are prepared for the worst. These women are trained in all the tools and tactics they need. The Lower Zambezi, one of the largest elephant populations left on the continent, had eight thousand elephants killed in the last sixteen years. That's eight thousand teams of armed men moving through there, [teams] who are willing and able to kill either rangers or the animals. And our women have to be prepared to meet them.

The teams have made sixty-two arrests since October [2017]. And these are not just low-level arrests. These are from the syndicates. And all of those arrests have been made without a shot being fired. It makes sense that the women form informal communications networks in those rural societies. That's a polite way of saying gossip. But they are really plugged into everything that's going on, and so most of the crimes are solved through coffee shop intelligence operations.

And finally, the communities are on our side. It's much easier to take a phone call or a text message from somebody in the local community—telling you about where a problem is—than it is to walk around a million acres looking for one.

MARK: What does the name Akashinga mean, and how did it come about?

DAMIEN: It's a name that the women came up with for themselves. It translates into "The Brave Ones." I thought, *Well, if we're going to recruit these women, let's give the ones that are the most oppressed an opportunity.* So the recruitment was open to victims of serious sexual assault, domestic violence, AIDS orphans, single wives, abandoned mothers, those types. And there have been no handouts on this course—they saw an opportunity and they made the most of it.

MARK: How do you recruit? Do you put a poster up and say, "Hey, if you've been sexually assaulted, we want to talk to you"? I can't imagine that working out.

DAMIEN: By bush telegraph! These are very tight-knit communities. Everyone knows everyone's business—so we went and spoke with the chief and said this is what we want to do. They were skeptical at first. This is perceived to be a man's job in a male-dominated culture. We managed to convince them, and they were very good in helping us open up that opportunity.

The second reserve will start in Kenya early next year. And once we have it running and functioning, and succeeding in a third reserve, we'll then make all the doctrine available for free to other organizations that agree to meet our standards.

While the West has helped drive a downturn in trophy hunting, we now need to look at alternatives to conservation by building communities that protect their own land. And from an economic standpoint, our program appears to be an appealing alternative.

MARK: I think empowering women to protect these areas, uplift their communities, support their families, and protect wildlife is a much more sellable market than trophy hunting.

DAMIEN: You know, when I sit down at the end of it all—on the porch somewhere in my rocking chair—I just want to look back and know that I helped play a part in building teams that were able to protect as much of the natural world as possible. We've got this amazing planet—this blue rock spinning through space—and we keep looking for miracles out there. When in actual fact the miracles are all around us here, in nature. And I think protecting it is a worthy mission. It has given me relevance, and it is giving the women relevance too. We need to give nature another chance. She will surprise us.

MARK: I couldn't agree more. You are protecting the environment and the animals, and empowering women to be the protectors. It's such a virtuous loop that you're creating—a very intriguing model for other industries. Getting ego-driven men to either transcend their ego, or step aside and let women have a go at the leading for once.

In a follow-up conversation, Damien updated me on his progress with the female teams.

DAMIEN: The ecosystems that balance our climate and make life on Earth possible are under extreme threat. Without sufficient action and along with humankind, we are destined to take millions of species to extinction. There has never been a more critical issue in civilization than the immediate protection of the natural world.

Putting women at the center of the conservation strategy is a simple yet innovative solution that can shift empowerment, development, and philanthropy across the African continent. From what I have now learned, I believe that beyond Akashinga, women will change the world for the better. As we scale toward a legion of a thousand vegan women protecting Africa's ecosystem by 2025, I can't think of a more empowering program to drive this message. What excites me are the possibilities. We started a trial in a small landlocked country of sub-

Saharan Africa, in a conservation industry that is becoming increasingly antagonistic with local indigenous communities, on a continent that has a 700 percent increase in armed conflict in the past decade. All we did was shift the male roles to construction and labor and put women into the power roles of law enforcement, management, and decision-making. In doing so, we completely de-escalated local tension and brought conservation and community together, while cutting our operational costs by two-thirds. The remaining third, invested mostly in women, becomes the most effective form of community development, while our core business of conservation is more successful than ever.

For so long we had been blinded by our egos from seeing the most powerful force in nature. That is a woman's instinct to protect. Where history is scarred with the battlefields of ego, women have remained the mothers, providers, and protectors of families. Binding society together, they bring stability to chaos. The hour of crisis has arrived, and eight centuries since Genghis Khan's men shook the world, it is now being shaken again for the better—only this time by a very different kind of force, a special one. Women.

Hooyah, Damien! I like your vision.

THE FATE OF HUMANITY DEPENDS ON YOU

What does it mean to be human now, as we race into the era of AI, robots, mass distraction, and growing existential threats? Like Damien, how do we find greater purpose, relevance, and a more significant mission in a world gone somewhat mad?

Yuval Noah Harari, the author of *Sapiens: A Brief History of Humankind,* claims that we are no longer as a species capable of dealing with the threats we have created. Nuclear war, ecological collapse, and technological disruption threaten to erase humanity. Yuval posits that these threats are problems that can be solved only by a global civilization, which we do not have. We are separated by national, cultural, and religious idealism and driven by rigid egocentric and ethnocentric world views. What we're doing doesn't seem to be working and could be a recipe for more suffering in the future.

But how do we come together to end separation? Many expected that the internet and global mobile access would usher in a global community. That promise faded a few years ago.

Can new technology such as blockchain, space exploration, and green energy solve the problems? Technology will undoubtedly extend life, colonize planets, maybe even end poverty—perhaps even begin to heal the planet. Yet it will also give us even more powerful tools to destroy ourselves. As a species separated from our own true nature, and thus from each other, we will continue to use these increasingly powerful weapons against "the others." We will continue to act in our own self-interests, in spite of the negative global consequences of our actions.

Separation from our true nature, and Mother Nature, has pitted us against one another in an endless fight for resources, territory, and power. Isolation, racial and sexual judgment, absolutist thinking, pillaging the Earth, despotic and radical behavior—all stem from separation. Separation creates fear, greed, gluttony, depression, sadness, anxiety, anger, and confusion. In a nutshell, separation causes suffering, which is played out culturally on the worldwide stage. Everyone is desperately seeking answers outside themselves in the next new leader, in academia, in the media hype or latest self-help course. They never find what they are looking for. There is no formal education on how to end separation and eliminate suffering. So everyone bounces from one drama to another, repeating deeply grooved religious, social, and family myths along the way.

To end separation from others, we must first end it in ourselves. We must stare down the fear wolf, wake up to our innate goodness and connection to one another, and reach the integrated fifth plateau of development. So, yeah, the fate of humanity *does* depend upon you. And me. The way to global wholeness is to first become whole ourselves.

This book is my way of motivating you to reframe your role as a leader (and teammate) for the future, which is now. That role is to develop agile and vertically developing teams and organizations that will lead the way for social and environmental reform—embodying the change as a leader of leaders, on one team of teams, with one common mission: *to win back our future.*

The industrial age bureaucracies and conglomerates, though well intentioned in most cases, have lost the right to lead in this new era. And the media will continue to obsess about the shadow side of culture and politics, fostering social negativity and unrest. That leaves you and me to move the dial in a positive, world-centric direction.

Within the next twenty years, we will most likely be an interplanetary species, with an outpost on the moon and Mars. How will we serve as stewards of our home planet in the shift to an interplanetary species? Do we do things the same way and pray for more positive results? Do we wait for a few brilliant entrepreneurs to solve things? Personally, I don't think either of these approaches will work. What I think is that you and I need to expand our potential and our conception of what we are capable of. Then we need to bring this expanding power to our teams and organizations. That is the only way not to get blown over like the mighty oak in the coming technological tsunami.

The accelerating technological advancements will soon make our planet feel very small. As a result of the work that you and I will do, I have a vision that we will reach a tipping point in the next ten to twenty years, when over 10 percent of humanity will identify themselves both as a member of their tribe *and* simultaneously as a citizen of the human race. That means they will demand equal rights, freedoms, and respectability for all. They will also demand that countries stop investing in violence and heal the environment at a gobal, and local level. I see breathing, meditation, visualization, and heart-mind skills taught in grade school, and humanity moving rapidly in a more positive direction as a result.

There is simply no future that makes sense with a continuing threat of nuclear, economic, or environmental annihilation. The days of scarcity and "my tribe is better than yours" needs to end. Only when enough teams and leaders share the truths of the seven commitments can we take over the dominant leadership roles and bully pulpits. Then together we can transform cultural and social structures to rebalance the collective body, mind, and spirit of humanity, as well as our home base, Earth.

It is your time to step into your role as a change agent, leading your audacious mission by example. You will make the biggest impact through your elite teams, embracing the seven commitments. The team is your vehicle to change, where you will lead with an open heart and hand, like the Akashinga women. Minds and hearts merged in bold action that goes beyond the bottom line—but does not ignore the bottom line.

Let's stare down the wolf of fear together and fight for our communities, planet Earth itself, and all of humanity. Take a sober look at the version of the future where you and I take no action. It's not pretty. So, let's commit to co-creating that alternative positive (probable!) future. Only by taking back our personal power can we stare down the negative forces that dominate today.

It is time for us to step into the breach.

Finally, there is a growing expectation from our youngest generation that the organizations they join will be part of the solution, not perpetuate the problems of the past. We need to give our young teammates something to mobilize around. Ask how your team and organization is going to make a difference. Commit to developing courage, trust, respect, growth, excellence, resiliency, and alignment to unlock massive potential.

Together we can do it. One team, one fight. We've got this—easy day!

STARE DOWN THAT FRIGGIN WOLF

Fear holds us back. You can step into your moral and physical courage by taking on the first commitment. Stare down your fears and simultaneously fuel courage. This will propel you naturally to take on the other six commitments. Courage develops from taking a stand and risking bold action. In fact, each of the seven commitments is a call to action. Each builds upon the other.

Without courage, you won't trust. If you don't trust, you won't get respect and won't respect others. If you don't respect yourself and others, then you won't grow. If you're not growing, then you won't express excellence. If you don't commit to excellence, then you won't be very resilient. Finally, if you're not resilient, then your team will have difficulty aligning with your vision or mission.

Staring down the wolf requires daily work to evolve your body, mind, and spirit. Embrace the suck of that work, get comfortable with discomfort, and learn to appreciate the accelerated growth that will come from it.

On the journey, remember these three things:

1. Self-mastery is an **EVERYDAY** practice. We must take ownership of our own evolution. This will stoke your courage and breathe fire into your other commitments.

2. This is not just about you. Every time you do the work, you are impacting your team, and humanity, positively. Check your ego and do this for the team.

3. **You must discover your unique calling and serve from that place. Humanity needs your unique skills and world-centric care.**

These commitments, then, are daily practices as well as powerful guiding principles to live by. Let's review the core practices and principles of each commitment.

COURAGE

When it comes to courage, stare down the fear of risk to stand up for truth—both the universal truth and your own. A key universal truth to stand for is inclusiveness and interconnectedness. If we are to be world-centric, we cannot deny, demonize, or judge other people's realities. We cannot be self-righteous. We have to let go of judgment and self-righteousness to be inclusive and respect the worthiness of others.

We also need to have the courage to follow our calling and not do things because other people think they're right, or because our parents wanted us to do them, or whatever the case may be. To be courageous means that we won't work for assholes and we won't do things that feed only our ego-oriented goals, as I did with the Coronado Brewing Company. I went into the CBC with the goals of making a ton of money and having free beer for life. Look how that turned out. That was not a very courageous act.

Courage requires that we practice expanding our risk tolerance and lead with the heart, as Olson demonstrated. In order to do that, we have to train to open the heart. One of the best ways I know to do that is to force yourself to have those critical, compassionate conversations every day. We all have those that we know we "should" do, but we avoid them until they "go away." They never really go away, though, do they? You can develop the courage to have those conversations just by committing to one a day. Doing so will train your heart to open up to others in mutual connectedness. You will be expanding your capacity for risk and sharing an important experience, which will develop greater trust and respect. These commitments all tie together like that.

TRUST

Stare down the fear of failure to commit to becoming trustworthy. That means you must develop transparency, humility, and the discipline to relentlessly follow through, the way McRaven did. Don't hide behind inaction or blame others or the situation when things don't go as planned. Doubt is eliminated through action and learning, but first and most important comes action. One of most powerful actions to cultivate trust is to admit your mistakes. Hiding behind my mistake in Arena Adventures led to a serious breach in my trustworthiness, which broke down the trust of the team.

Own your mistakes day in and day out. Don't just acknowledge them to yourself, but declare them loudly and humbly to the team. Say, "Hey, folks, I screwed this up. Clearly I am not perfect! I hope it doesn't impact us too bad. I need your help fixing things up." It sounds so simple, but it can be so hard to say the first few times. We were taught that messing up is bad. That's bullshit. It is how we learn together. You want to quickly get to the heart of authenticity? Tell everyone when you fuck up, then go on to say that you're working on fixing things and improving. People will start to trust you quickly when you do this.

RESPECT

Stare down your fear of judgment and get really clear about your why and your mission. Clarify your specific and implied objectives, and what acceptable victory and failure looks like. Then communicate these with disciplined integrity and a moral compass. No plan will survive VUCA, so to navigate it intact, you have to be clear about why you're doing what you're doing at each step of the way. Otherwise, you will lose respect quickly. Communicate to the team that ultimate victory won't look anything like what you originally thought, and that is okay. It is how the team responds to the challenges and changes, and how adaptable the team members are, that will determine success. In the SEALs, an acceptable victory was also that we learned how *not* to do something in the future. We didn't always have to get the mission done as prescribed, which gave us a ton of flexibility to keep driving forward.

You have to earn your respect every single day, and you do that with communication steeped in integrity, as I saw with Captain O'Connell. That means removing your masks and speaking with the three-part intention introduced there—that what you say is factually true, that it's helpful and adds to the conversation, and that it comes from a place of positivity.

As far as those masks are concerned, if you wear them, you lose respect, because the team will see through immediately. The most important mask to shed is the mask of perfection, which is born from fear. I outsourced NavySEALs.com in its earliest days due to my own masking of fear. I didn't trust my competency and feared that I couldn't do it by myself—that I needed these people to fill that gap. That codependence came from my childhood sense of not being worthy. When I gained the self-awareness and courage to stare it down, it went away. If I had done that emotional work and shed that mask earlier in my life, I could have saved a ton of time, money, and suffering. I also lacked the integrity of the three-part communication to get through it gracefully, and the whole thing was a disaster. I lost respect for them and they lost respect for me.

Respect is gained slowly, but lost quickly.

Face every opportunity to drop the masks. Do this every day, and respect will be impossible to deny.

GROWTH

Stare down the fear of discomfort by embracing the challenge of vertical character development—for both you and your team. Practicing the seven commitments with your team will create an engine for unbelievable growth. You need to become the person worthy of guiding your team as a world-centric leader, like the Horra became through his own commitment to growth. Why would you give up eight to ten hours of your day to "work" (more for many of you), and not demand that the time provide a major growth opportunity for you?

You will want to systematize challenge and variety and find

more mentors—not just one, but a team of mentors and coaches. Also be a mentor-coach to others.

Everyone needs a mentor, and in more than one category. You'll need one for your physical development, your mental development, your business or entrepreneurship needs, your emotional development, and your spiritual development. It's quite difficult to find all of that support in one person.

When I look back and compare my peace of mind and results when I was committed to growth and had mentors, to my peace of mind and results when I wasn't, the difference is glaring. I slid off the rails quickly when I was distracted by all the doing, ignoring the work on my being. For example, I ended up with CBC, with Arena Adventures, and with the early NavySEALs.com debacles all because I had "paused" my inner work. After my combat tour with the SEALs in Iraq, I committed to never prioritize achievement over growth. I took this even further when I discovered that teaching these principles was my calling.

Better to seek peace of mind than glory or fortune.

When I started SEALFIT, I made the daily integrated training of physical, mental, emotional, intuitive, and spiritual skills part of the training model, and I led that training by example. I got back into the martial arts, back into meditation and yoga—and committed to practicing every day, rain or shine, for at least an hour. Everything changed for the better. If you commit to daily vertical growth, you will make great strides, and quickly. The challenges won't go away, but you'll have new perspectives and resiliency, and will respond positively. The minute you stop training, the well-worn negative patterns will reappear again. The fear wolf does not leave your head. He will just lie there and wait for an opportunity to be noticed again.

Commit to growth by training daily in these commitments, doing "hard" every day, and changing it up frequently. Keep things fresh so you never get too comfortable.

EXCELLENCE

Stare down the fear of being seen as unique, instead seek to develop curiosity, innovation, and simplicity. Excellence is first found on the inside, and then expressed through your character and actions. This requires that you embrace silence and the practices that cultivate simplicity, curiosity, and innovation. Excellence is not so much a way of acting as a way of being.

The team needs to take time to come together and train this commitment—inside and outside the office. Start to do things together to get comfortable with discomfort. Plan periodic retreats and time off to reflect, restore, and deepen insight and gain important new perspectives.

Embody excellence first and then transmit it through your actions.

When you commit to excellence by embracing the practices daily rather than as concepts, you and your team become your own "SEAL Team Six." Develop your character to be morally courageous, trustworthy, and respectable first, then go accomplish your mission with excellence. Your "basic training" is to carve out fifteen to thirty minutes each morning. During this time do five to ten minutes of deep diaphragmatic box breathing (Google "mark divine box breathing"), followed by five to ten minutes of mindfulness; finish by journaling the patterns and ideas that came up. Create a team practice of box breathing, visualization, and feeding the courage wolf.

RESILIENCY

Stare down your fear of the big obstacles. Fall down seven times, get up eight—stronger and with a smile on your face. It's often said that we need to adapt and overcome, but I suggest that we overcome, and then adapt. Overcome the obstacles first, then learn to adapt from the experience to be more resilient and wiser.

Embody accelerated learning so that you can "run toward the sound of gunfire"—that is, toward the obstacles and challenges. Learn how to learn fast and acknowledge that you're capable of at least twenty times more than you think you are. Then, go out and prove it. Expect obstacles, then persistently blow through them one at a time, employing crisis leadership, the OODA loop, and other tools discussed in this book.

A mantra I use often is "Day by day, in every way, I'm getting stronger and better. Hooyah-hey."

Hooyah is the SEAL warrior shout that brings the team together in the spirit of "we got this, no problem." This and my other mantras keep me positive and optimistic and help me cultivate resiliency. Don't be afraid to be a white belt again. Empty your cup to allow for new ideas and energy to flow in. Be willing to show up every day with a fresh start, a beginner's mind.

ALIGNMENT

Stare down the fear of sharing your self fully. Learn to share everything worth sharing. Open yourself to sharing exposure to risk, reward, and the experience of the whole team. Get out of the box, out of the office, and out of your head. Be authentic by connecting to your heart and then the heart of your team. Ask what's going well, what is not working, and what you can do to help. Get involved in cross-functional teams, task forces, or think tanks. Risk not being the expert, then become one. Ask to lead things that scare you. If you're the leader, share your visions and expectations and get relentless with your battle comms to get everyone in sync with the mission.

Everyone's got a unique skill. Don't hide yours or squash others. And when it's "all hands on deck," be willing to pick up a hammer and take out the trash. There's nothing worse than a specialist who holds back, thinking, *That's not MY job.* Commit to developing the team's shared sense of meaning, like McChrystal did with his team of teams.

Develop a deeply meaningful morning ritual, one that will allow you to win in your mind before you start the day, both as an individual and as a team. Learn from your mistakes and eradicate regrets in your evening ritual.

Live life "one day, one life" at a time.

Courage begets trust; trust begets respect; respect leads to growth; growth leads to excellence; excellence forges resiliency; and resiliency gives you the stick-to-itiveness and the power to constantly align with your team. That way, together, you can radically focus on the who and the why as well as the what and the how of your missions.

This is how teams grow together and how you grow to be a leader worthy of their support. Who you are as a teammate, who the team is as a whole, and why we all do what we do are paramount. Figure out your collective why and how you want to be together as a team first. Then determine how you will change the world together.

Together, as one team we will win this fight. Staring down the wolf. Hooyah!

UNBEATABLE MIND

What would your team or business be like if everyone had an Unbeatable Mind as described in this book? If everyone had the mental toughness, the resilience, and the emotional awareness forged by Unbeatable Mind training?

How would your business be different if everyone was focused on the team and elevating others around them? If they lived the seven commitments that forge elite teams? If your team embodied courage, trust, respect, growth, excellence, resiliency, and alignment?

What would it be like if every team member had the courage to face their own biases, patterns, and conditioning that prevents them from being heart-centered leaders and teammates?

The good news is that you don't have to wonder. You can bring Unbeatable Mind into your organization. Unbeatable Mind coaches can help your team stare down their fear wolf.

ACKNOWLEDGMENTS

When my publisher asked me to author a book about SEAL leadership, I didn't want to re-tread ground already well rutted about the secrets of leadership from the world's most badass warriors. Some of my teammates, and even I, had already written those books.

Yes, SEALs are incredibly effective on the battlefield. When the bullets are flying these operators are in their element, making leading look easy. But my experience is that reading about leading a SEAL team in VUCA, though exciting storytelling, doesn't suddenly transform a corporate executive or entrepreneur in to an "elite leader." Something big is missing.

The reality is that the system and culture of the SEALs makes leading in that environment kind of easy. But when I left the service to build an entrepreneurial team, and later at corporate team, I was without that extraordinary structure and culture to back me up, to cover for my many flaws. I was on my own, with my new team, who couldn't care less how effective I was a leading other SEALs. Soon my ego and shadow tripped me up.

So, my first acknowledgment goes to all those teammates—from the very start of my entrepreneurial journey—who helped expose my shadow and limitations. I want to especially thank those who still consider me their "enemy" to this day. Without the suffering I would be half the man I am today.

Thank you Michael Homler of St. Martin's Press for believing in me and allowing me to do this project my way. Thanks to John Vercher of Scribe for suggesting the epic title, which cornered me into writing the book that I needed to write.

Thanks to all of my living teachers and mentors, especially Tadashi Nakamura, Ken Wilber, Dan Brown, Gary Kraftsow, Sean Esbjorne-Hargrove, Christie Turner, and the Hoffman Institute team who have all been instrumental in helping me stare down my own wolf of fear.

My heartfelt gratitude to all the SEALs that I profiled in the book including Admiral William McRaven, Admiral Eric Olson, Captain Jim O'Connell, Master Chief "the Horra," Commander Richard Marcinko, Hospital Corpsman First Class Marcus Luttrell, and Master Chief Mike Magaraci. If I missed the mark with any of the stories, then I apologize and owe you burpees and a beer.

Thanks to the companies and individuals who helped me with insights and quotes, including: Joe De Sena of Spartan Racing, the Space X and Harvard Med Neurosurgeon teams, Christian Overton and the Shell GOM Deepwater team, Mohi Ahmed and the OIG team at Fujitsu, and Sheldon Wizotski at TGG. I appreciate your tremendous support and willingness to be included in the book.

Thanks to my elite team of Jim Brault, Melanie Swiwka, Geoff Haskell, Michael Ostrolenk, Richard Thompson, Mark Crampton, Robert Ord, Jon Atwater, Will Potter, Allison Glader and Tara Trainor for your amazing and loyal support.

Much love to my mom and dad, Brad, Charlie, and Robin, who provided me with the experiences that would allow me to be an effective SEAL leader, as well as the grist for my shadow work.

Finally, I would like to thank my family who inspires me to stay on the path of growth and staring down the wolf. May I have the strength to show up authentically and in presence every day. I love you Sandy, Cindy, Catherine, Devon, Rich, Wilder, Violet and Danger, Larry and Starlight.

ABOUT THE AUTHOR

MARK DIVINE

Mark Divine is the founder and CEO of the Courage Foundation, a 501c(3) supporting Vets with PTS. A Navy SEAL officer, successful serial entrepreneur, bestselling author, and leadership development expert, he graduated as honor man from his SEAL BUD/S class 170 and served nine years on active duty and eleven years as a reserve SEAL before retiring as commander in 2011. His career as a business entrepreneur includes cofounding the Coronado Brewing Company and founding and leading the internationally known SEALFIT and Unbeatable Mind companies that provide leadership training, coaching, and elite team development. Mark is the *New York Times* bestselling author of *The Way of the SEAL: Think Like an Elite Warrior to Lead and Succeed*; *8 Weeks to SEALFIT: A Navy SEAL's Guide to Unconventional Training for Physical and Mental Toughness*; *Unbeatable Mind*; and *Kokoro Yoga*. Mark hosts the top-ranked *Unbeatable Mind* podcast. He lives in Leucadia, California.

FREE
LEADERSHIP ASSESSMENT

Discover Your
7 Unique Commitments

Just go to **StaringDownTheWolf.com**
and enter **code: 73p99** to take the
7 commitments leadership assessment.

After you complete the assessment,
you will receive a personalized
7 commitments leadership guide.

*This offer is valid for one use per book only.

INDEX